PICKY EATER
COOKBOOK

84 Fun & Easy Recipes Kids Will Actually Eat

CENTENNIAL KITCHEN®

CENTENNIAL BOOKS

PICKY EATER
COOKBOOK

84 Fun & Easy Recipes Kids Will Actually Eat

103
Strawberry Cupcakes
With Strawberry
Buttercream Frosting

CONTENTS

keep your eye out!
Our fork-and-spoon
logo shows you
which recipes
are our healthy
picks.

89
Cheeseburgers
With Crispy Sweet
Potato Fries

HOW TO PLEASE EVEN THE PICKIEST EATERS

Do you have a child who shrieks at the sight of spinach or cowers at the mention of cauliflower? Most kids are at least a little finicky when it comes to fresh fruits and vegetables. But when they get involved in the kitchen, suddenly mealtime becomes a lot more fun—even if what you're serving up is so-called healthy fare. Plus cooking is a hands-on activity that challenges kids' creativity and gives them a sense of accomplishment.

This book offers a wide variety of delicious recipes, plus opportunities for your youngsters to learn and grow. Something as simple as pouring ingredients into a bowl and stirring them together enhances hand-eye coordination. Reading recipes and packaging labels increases language skills. And measuring flour, milk and spices helps kids understand fractions and lets them put their addition and subtraction knowledge to use. Best yet, cooking together provides you with a wonderful way to spend time with your children and introduce them to healthy eating habits.

Discover more than 80 kid-approved ideas for every meal of the day, plus snacks and party foods. Children will have a blast making Confetti Waffles (p. 17) for a weekend breakfast, planting vegetable dippers in their Black Bean Dip Garden (p. 61) as a snack or discovering new dishes from around the globe (p. 78). There are even recipes specially designed to help Mom and Dad sneak extra nutrition into favorite foods like mac and cheese and pizza (p. 88), along with tips for creating take-to-school lunches that won't be traded or thrown away when lunchtime rolls around (p. 42). And, of course, dessert—from bake-sale goodies (p. 98) you'll want to save for yourself to the best birthday cakes ever (p. 104).

The recipe for success begins with knowing the basics. To help budding young chefs master their skills, each of the cooking-together recipes in this book includes a tool list along with easy-to-understand directions. There's also a dictionary of common kitchen terms and a guide that shows the right tools for the job.

More than just another recipe guide, *Picky Eater Cookbook* will not only help your family build basic kitchen skills—it will also help you and your little ones create memories to last a lifetime!

SS

Cauli Crust
Pepperoni Pizza

LET'S GET COOKIN'

CHOOSE A RECIPE, GRAB THE INGREDIENTS AND FIND THE
RIGHT TOOLS. IT'S TIME TO WHIP UP SOME FUN IN THE KITCHEN!

A little
planning
helps keep
things
enjoyable.

Before You Begin

Cooking with kids can be a rewarding experience. It can also be messy and frustrating if you're not prepared. Here are some ideas for making your time together fun for the kids—and you!

Be Enthusiastic

If you enjoy cooking, eating and being in the kitchen, chances are your child will acquire that same enthusiasm along with you.

Set Aside a Special Time

Spending time in the kitchen with your child doesn't need to be an everyday activity. Choose one recipe a week to prepare together. During the rest of the week, ask your child to help with some simple tasks while you're preparing meals, such as washing produce or setting the table.

Plan Together

Planning is half the fun. Ask your child to choose a recipe, and together make a list of ingredients needed from the store or that you already have at home.

Keep It Safe

Create a safe kitchen by providing low stools so younger children can reach things. Use utensils that fit their hands. Remove sharp objects from their reach and provide age-appropriate rules about the stove.

Choose the Right Tasks

Kids have different abilities and experiences with preparing food. Choose tasks that are appropriate for their age and skill level. You can start out with simple tasks such as spreading butter and jams, then move up to more challenging jobs, like cracking eggs or sifting dry ingredients (see p. 10).

HEY PARENTS!

Give kids tasks they can do so they don't get frustrated—and neither will you!

Make Cleanup Part of the Process

Start with tasks like putting a jellyroll pan underneath a bowl to catch spills and wearing aprons to help make cleanup easier. Also, while you're cooking, teach kids that throwing away trash, putting dishes into the dishwasher and wiping up messes are all part of the cooking process.

Relax and Enjoy!

Try to keep cooking with your child light and fun, and be patient with spills and mistakes. The goal of cooking together is to enjoy your time with each other.

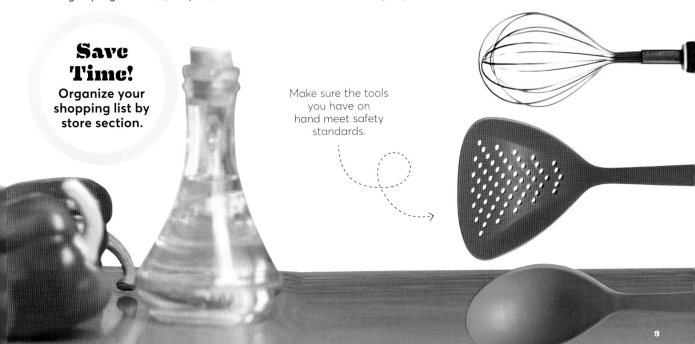

Save Time!

Organize your shopping list by store section.

Make sure the tools you have on hand meet safety standards.

Kids are much more likely to eat foods they make.

Kids Can Help Cook at Any Age

To encourage culinary interest and excitement, choose kitchen activities appropriate to your child's age and abilities.

2- to 3-year-olds
- Wipe tabletops
- **Wash fruits and vegetables**
- Tear lettuce and salad greens
- **Carry unbreakable items to the table**
- Stir ingredients in large, deep bowls
- **Spread butters or soft toppings**
- Put things into the trash

4- to 5-year-olds
- **Dry lettuce greens in a salad spinner**
- Squeeze citrus using a plastic juicer
- **Measure ingredients**
- Beat eggs with an egg beater
- **Shake together ingredients in a closed container**
- Cut soft foods with a table or plastic knife
- **Sift dry ingredients**
- Set the table

6- to 8-year-olds
- Find ingredients in the pantry and refrigerator
- **Peel potatoes, apples or other vegetables and fruits with a peeler**
- Crack eggs into a bowl
- **Grease pans**
- Form patties
- **Scoop cookie dough onto cookie sheets and roll dough into balls**
- Help make school lunch the night before

9- to 10-year-olds
- **Follow simple recipes**
- Prepare meals with few items
- **Use small appliances**
- Microwave foods
- **Prepare cakes and brownies from mixes**
- Make pancakes and waffles
- **Roll and cut out cookie dough**

COOKING WORDS

Bake Cook food in an oven.

Beat Add air or make a mixture smooth by mixing ingredients with a fork, a spoon or an electric mixer.

Boil Heat liquids on the stove until big bubbles form and break the surface quickly.

Broil Cook food directly under the heat source in an oven.

Chill Refrigerate food until it gets cold.

Chop Use a knife to cut food into small pieces.

Cool Let food sit on the counter until it is no longer hot.

Cover Put plastic wrap or foil over the food so air does not dry it out. Also, put a lid on a saucepan so the food cooks faster.

Drain Pour food in a colander or strainer to remove the liquid.

Drizzle Slowly pour spoonfuls of liquid over food in thin streams.

Grate Scrape food against the holes of a grater to make small pieces.

Grease Lightly spread a thin layer of oil, butter or shortening on the inside of a baking pan or dish to prevent food from sticking.

Mash Smash food with a fork, a spoon or a potato masher.

Melt Apply heat to a solid food to turn it into a liquid.

Mix Stir food with a fork, spoon or electric mixer until it looks the same all the way through.

Preheat Turn on the oven or broiler ahead of time so it will be heated to the necessary temperature for cooking the food.

Simmer Heat liquids on the stove until small bubbles form and gently break the surface.

Slice Use a knife to cut food into thin pieces.

Thread Push small pieces of food onto a stick, called a skewer.

Whisk The same as beat, except using a wire whisk as the tool.

HEY KIDS!

Ready, Set, Cook!

Your culinary adventure awaits. But before you put on your apron, here are a few kitchen basics you need to know.

☐ Read the recipe from start to finish—the ingredients, tool lists and all the directions.

☐ Ask a grown-up to explain any words, cooking steps or foods that are unfamiliar to you.

☐ Gather all the ingredients and tools before you start cooking.

☐ Wear an apron to keep your clothes clean. Also, tie back your hair, remove any loose jewelry and roll up your sleeves.

☐ Wash your hands. Even if they look clean, you still need to wash them to get rid of germs and bacteria. Wash for at least 20 seconds with lots of soapy water. Remember to also wash the backs of your hands, fingers and fingernails.

Safety First!
Minimize knife use until kids are clearly ready.

TOOLS OF THE TRADE

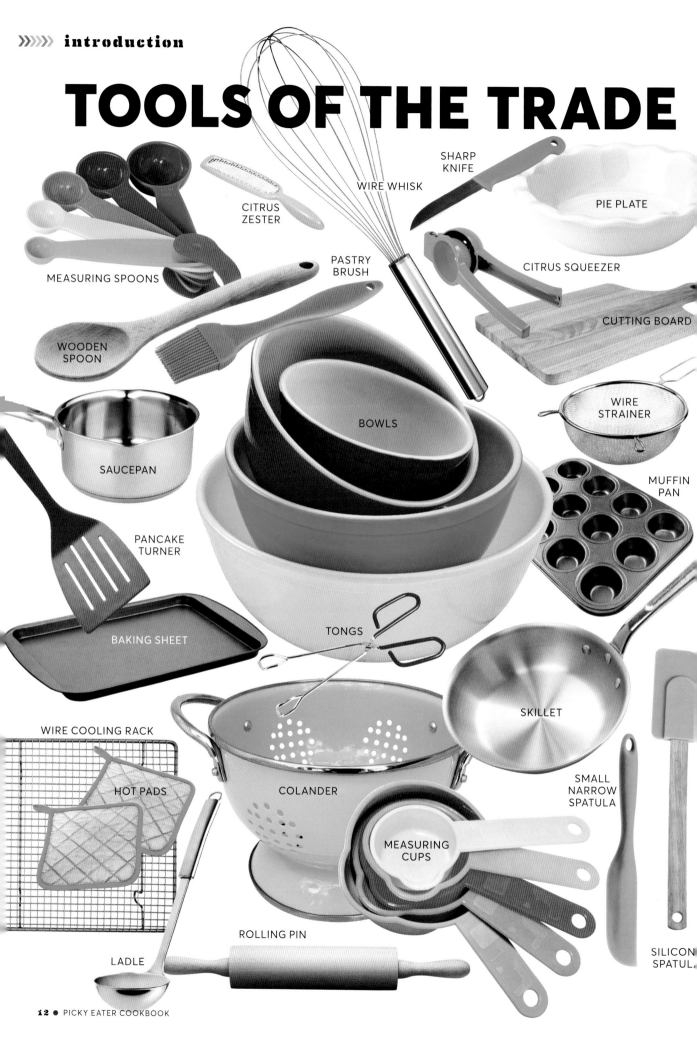

MEASURING SPOONS

CITRUS ZESTER

WIRE WHISK

SHARP KNIFE

PIE PLATE

CITRUS SQUEEZER

CUTTING BOARD

PASTRY BRUSH

WOODEN SPOON

BOWLS

WIRE STRAINER

SAUCEPAN

MUFFIN PAN

PANCAKE TURNER

BAKING SHEET

TONGS

SKILLET

WIRE COOLING RACK

COLANDER

SMALL NARROW SPATULA

HOT PADS

MEASURING CUPS

LADLE

ROLLING PIN

SILICON SPATUL

Teamwork makes the dream work! Have fun and learn together.

High Five for Safety Smarts

1 Always wash your hands, cutting boards, countertops, dishes and silverware with warm soapy water immediately after cutting and handling raw foods like meats, poultry and seafood.

2 Use one cutting board and knife for fresh produce and another board and knife for raw meats, poultry and seafood.

3 Keep raw foods separate from cooked foods. Never use the same plate.

4 Use a thermometer to make sure meats, poultry and fish are cooked to a safe temperature. Have a grown-up help you with sticking a cooking thermometer into the center of hot foods.

5 Refrigerate or freeze any leftovers immediately after you're done eating. Perishable food should not be kept at room temperature for more than 2 hours.

KITCHEN MATH

HEY KIDS! Use your fraction skills when measuring ingredients.

SPOONS

¼ teaspoon = ¼ teaspoon

½ teaspoon = ¼ teaspoon + ¼ teaspoon

¾ teaspoon = ½ teaspoon + ¼ teaspoon

1 teaspoon = ¼ teaspoon + ¼ teaspoon +
¼ teaspoon + ¼ teaspoon **or**
½ teaspoon + ½ teaspoon

1 tablespoon = 1 teaspoon + 1 teaspoon + 1 teaspoon

CUPS

¼ cup = 1 tablespoon + 1 tablespoon + 1 tablespoon + 1 tablespoon

½ cup = ¼ cup + ¼ cup

⅔ cup = ⅓ cup + ⅓ cup

¾ cup = ¼ cup + ¼ cup + ¼ cup

1 cup = ½ cup + ½ cup **or**
⅓ cup + ⅓ cup + ⅓ cup **or**
¼ cup + ¼ cup + ¼ cup + ¼ cup

» › **chapter 1** ‹ «

MMM... MORNINGS

BEGIN YOUR DAY WITH ONE OF THESE
FUN-TO-MAKE AND FUN-TO-EAT BREAKFASTS.

17
Confetti
Waffles

START YOUR ENGINES!

GIVE YOUR FAMILY THE FUEL THEY NEED FOR ACTION-PACKED DAYS.

Wake up to party waffles!

Confetti Waffles

MAKES 6 SERVINGS

WHAT YOU NEED

Nonstick cooking spray
2 cups all-purpose flour
½ cup white sugar
2 teaspoons baking powder
½ teaspoon salt
2 eggs
1 cup milk
⅓ cup canola oil
2 teaspoons vanilla extract
½ cup rainbow sprinkles
GARNISHES: maple or fruit pancake syrup; sweetened whipped cream; additional rainbow sprinkles

HOW TO MAKE IT

1 Spray grids of waffle iron with nonstick spray, then preheat waffle iron.
2 In a large bowl, place flour, sugar, baking powder and salt. Use a wire whisk to stir until mixed.
3 In a medium bowl, place eggs, milk, oil and vanilla. Use a wire whisk to stir until mixed. Make a hole in center of flour mixture. Pour egg mixture into flour mixture. Use a wooden spoon to stir just until mixed (batter will be slightly lumpy). Gently stir in sprinkles.
4 Use a ladle to scoop and pour a small amount of batter onto waffle iron. Close lid and cook 4 to 5 minutes.
5 Use fork to remove waffles from waffle iron. Place on serving plates. Serve with desired garnishes.

tools

Measuring cups • Measuring spoons • Waffle iron • Large bowl • Wire whisk • Medium bowl • Wooden spoon • Small ladle • Fork

Overnight Oatmeal

MAKES 1 SERVING

WHAT YOU NEED

½ cup old-fashioned rolled oats
⅔ cup reduced-fat milk or unsweetened coconut milk
⅓ cup plain Greek yogurt
1-2 tablespoons honey
½ tablespoon chia seeds
½ teaspoon vanilla extract
⅛ teaspoon salt
¼ cup sweetened flaked coconut
¼ cup chopped fresh pineapple
¼ cup chopped fresh mango

HOW TO MAKE IT

1 In a pint jar or small bowl, place oats, milk, yogurt, honey, chia seeds, vanilla and salt. Use a spoon to stir until well mixed.
2 Add coconut, pineapple and mango. Gently stir until mixed.
3 Place lid tightly on jar, or cover bowl tightly with plastic wrap. Refrigerate 5 hours or overnight.
4 Uncover oatmeal. Use a spoon to stir; serve chilled or warm in a microwave-safe jar or bowl if desired.

⇩

tools

Measuring cups •
Measuring spoons •
Sharp knife • Cutting
board • Pint jar with lid
or small bowl with
plastic wrap •
Spoon

Sprinkle with powdered sugar for decoration.

⬇

tools

Measuring cups • Measuring spoons • Sharp knife • Cutting board • 2 pie plates or shallow bowls • Wire whisk • Tongs • Griddle • Pancake turner

Cinnamon French Toast Sticks

MAKES 4 SERVINGS

WHAT YOU NEED

2 **eggs**
1 **cup half-and-half**
1 **teaspoon ground cinnamon**
1 **teaspoon vanilla extract**
   Pinch salt
2 **tablespoons white sugar**
8 **slices challah bread**
2 **tablespoons butter**
   GARNISHES: maple pancake syrup; powdered sugar

HOW TO MAKE IT

1 In a pie plate or shallow bowl, crack eggs. Add half-and-half, cinnamon, vanilla and salt. Use a wire whisk to stir until mixed.

2 In another pie plate or shallow bowl, place sugar.

3 Use a sharp knife to cut bread slices into thirds. Place a few bread pieces at a time into egg mixture. Using tongs, flip pieces to make sure all sides are well coated.

4 Remove bread pieces from egg mixture and place in sugar. Using tongs, flip pieces to make sure all sides are well coated.

5 On a griddle over medium heat, melt butter.

6 Place coated bread pieces on griddle. Cook 2 to 3 minutes or until golden brown; using a pancake turner, flip pieces and cook 2 to 3 minutes on other side. Place on serving plates. Serve with desired garnishes.

tools

Measuring cups • Measuring spoons • Citrus zester • Citrus squeezer • Sharp knife • Cutting board • Large resealable plastic bag • Bundt pan • Small saucepan • Wooden spoon • Hot pads • Wire cooling rack

Caramel Orange Monkey Bread

MAKES 12 SERVINGS

WHAT YOU NEED

- 4 (7.5-ounce) containers refrigerated buttermilk biscuit dough
- ½ cup white sugar
- 2 tablespoons finely shredded orange peel
  Pinch of salt
- 1 stick (½ cup) unsalted butter
- ½ cup packed light brown sugar
- ¼ cup fresh orange juice

HOW TO MAKE IT

1 Preheat oven to 350 F. Open biscuit containers; use a sharp knife to cut each biscuit into quarters.

2 In a large resealable plastic bag, place white sugar, orange peel and salt. Seal bag; shake until mixed. Open bag and add biscuit pieces. Seal bag; shake until pieces are coated.

3 Put pieces in a Bundt pan. Pour any sugar left in bag over biscuits.

4 In a small saucepan over medium heat, melt butter. Use a wooden spoon to stir in brown sugar and orange juice. Pour butter mixture over biscuit pieces in pan.

5 Bake 40 minutes or until tops of biscuits are golden brown. Use hot pads to remove pan from oven; place on wire cooling rack. After 10 minutes, turn pan over onto serving plate to remove bread. Let cool, then serve.

Ham and Cheese Omelet in a Bag

MAKES 2 SERVINGS

WHAT YOU NEED

- 4 eggs
- 1 cup shredded Italian cheese blend
- ½ cup chopped smoked ham
- ¼ cup chopped red onion
- ¼ cup chopped green bell pepper
- ¼ cup chopped tomato
   Salt and ground black pepper
- 2 tablespoons chopped fresh chives

tools

Measuring cups •
Measuring spoons •
Sharp knife • Cutting board •
Large saucepan • 2 quart
resealable plastic
freezer bags •
Tongs

HOW TO MAKE IT

1 In a large saucepan, add water until half full. Set stove to medium heat; bring water to a simmer.
2 Meanwhile, crack 2 eggs into each freezer bag. Press out as much air as you can. Seal bags.
3 Squeeze eggs in each bag until mixed. Carefully open one bag; add half of cheese, ham, onion, bell pepper and tomato to bag. Sprinkle with salt and pepper. Press out as much air as you can. Seal bag. Repeat with second bag and remaining ingredients. Roll tops of bags down, pushing egg mixture to bottom of bags.
4 Carefully place bags in simmering water. Simmer 8 minutes or until eggs are cooked. Use tongs to remove bags from water. Unseal bags and roll each omelet out onto a serving plate. Sprinkle with chives and serve.

Create your own veggie & cheese combo.

Blueberry Muffins

MAKES 12 MUFFINS

WHAT YOU NEED

Nonstick cooking spray
- 2 cups all-purpose flour
- ¾ cup white sugar
- 2 teaspoons baking powder
- ¼ teaspoon salt
- 2 eggs
- 1 cup milk
- 1 stick (½ cup) unsalted butter, melted
- 1 teaspoon vanilla extract
- 2 cups fresh or frozen blueberries

HOW TO MAKE IT

1 Preheat oven to 375 F. Lightly spray 12 (2½-inch) cups of a muffin pan with nonstick spray, or line with paper liners. Set aside.

2 In a large bowl, place flour, sugar, baking powder and salt. Use a wire whisk to stir until mixed.

3 In a medium bowl, place eggs, milk, butter and vanilla. Use a wire whisk to stir until mixed. Make a hole in center of flour mixture. Pour egg mixture into flour mixture. Use a wooden spoon to stir just until mixed (batter will be slightly lumpy). Gently stir in blueberries.

4 Use an ice cream scoop or spoon to scoop an equal amount of batter into each muffin cup.

5 Bake 15 to 20 minutes or until a toothpick inserted near the centers of the muffins comes out clean.

6 Use hot pads to remove pan from oven. Place pan on a wire cooling rack. Cool muffins in muffin cups for 5 minutes. Remove muffins from cups and serve warm or at room temperature.

tools

Measuring cups • Measuring spoons • Muffin pan (12 muffin cups) • Paper liners (optional) • Large bowl • Wire whisk • Medium bowl • Wooden spoon • Ice cream scoop or large spoon • Toothpick • Hot pads • Wire cooling rack

Use your favorite shaped cookie cutter!

tools

Measuring spoons •
2½- to 3-inch biscuit
or cookie cutter •
Large nonstick skillet
with lid • Custard cup •
Pancake turner

Sunshine Eggs in a Hole

MAKES 2 SERVINGS

WHAT YOU NEED

- 2 slices bread (whole wheat or white)
- 1 tablespoon butter
- 2 eggs
- ¼ teaspoon salt
- ⅛ teaspoon ground black pepper

HOW TO MAKE IT

1 Use biscuit or cookie cutter to cut a hole in center of each slice of bread.

2 In a skillet over medium-low heat, melt butter. Tilt skillet to coat entire bottom with butter.

3 Place bread slices in skillet. Cook 5 minutes or until they are lightly toasted. Use a pancake turner to turn bread slices over.

4 In a custard cup, carefully break 1 egg. Slide egg into cutout area of 1 bread slice. Repeat with remaining egg and bread. Cover skillet; cook 6 to 7 minutes or until eggs are firm and thoroughly cooked.

5 Use a pancake turner to place toasts on a serving plate. Sprinkle with salt and pepper; serve warm.

tools

Measuring cups • Measuring spoons • Griddle or skillet • Cutting board • Large bowl • Wire whisk • Medium bowl • Wooden spoon • Pastry brush • Ladle • Spoon • Pancake turner

Adorable Animal Pancakes

MAKES 12 TO 14 STANDARD-SIZE PANCAKES

WHAT YOU NEED

- 2 cups all-purpose flour
- 2 tablespoons baking powder
- ¼ teaspoon salt
- 4 eggs
- 3⅓ cups vanilla, banana or peach Greek yogurt
  Shortening
  GARNISHES: banana slices, kiwi slices, orange sections, apple slices, berries, raisins, chocolate chips, syrups, spreads (Nutella, peanut butter, jam)

HOW TO MAKE IT

1 In a large bowl, place flour, baking powder and salt. Use a wire whisk to stir until mixed.

2 In a medium bowl, place eggs and yogurt. Use a wire whisk to stir until mixed. Make a hole in center of flour mixture. Pour egg mixture into flour mixture. Use a wooden spoon to stir just until mixed (batter will be slightly lumpy).

3 Use a pastry brush to lightly brush griddle or skillet with shortening. Over medium-high heat, heat griddle. When griddle is hot, use a ladle to scoop some batter onto griddle. (Use ⅓ cup for large pancakes, ¼ cup for medium and 2 tablespoons for small pancakes; make some pancakes in each size, referring to photos for animal ideas.) Spread batter with back of spoon.

4 Cook pancakes over medium heat 1 to 2 minutes. When pancake surfaces become bubbly and edges are slightly dry, use pancake turner to flip pancakes; cook 1 to 2 minutes or until golden. Cook additional batches of pancakes in same manner.

5 Place pancakes on a serving platter.

6 Give everyone a plate so they can select several pancakes to assemble and decorate their animal face with garnishes, as desired.

A friendly lion has a mane of oranges.

This little piggy is yummy.

Go bananas for this monkey!

SO-GOOD SMOOTHIES

SO EASY TO MAKE—AND HEALTHY, TOO!
WHIP UP YOUR FAVORITE FRUIT SMOOTHIE FOR
AN ON-THE-GO BREAKFAST OR A SATISFYING SNACK.

This is yummy
and creamy!
ZOEY, AGE 4

Peachy Keen
Smoothie

Rocking Raspberry Smoothie

I could drink one of these every morning!
BENJI, AGE 7

Fruity Avocado Spinach Green Smoothie

TURN PAGE FOR RECIPES!

tools

Measuring cups • Measuring spoons • Table knife (for cutting soft bananas and avocados) • Cutting board • Blender Serving glasses

Blueberry Oat Smoothie

Strawberry Banana Smoothie

Strawberries and bananas are my favorite fruits!

EMMA, AGE 8

Strawberry Banana Smoothie

MAKES 2 TO 4 SERVINGS

WHAT YOU NEED

2½ cups frozen mixed sliced strawberries and bananas
2 cups reduced-fat milk
½ cup apple or orange juice
1 teaspoon honey

HOW TO MAKE IT

1 In a blender, place fruit, milk, juice and honey.
2 Cover and blend by turning blender on and off several times until mixture is smooth.
3 Pour smoothie into glasses and serve.

Peachy Keen Smoothie

MAKES 2 SERVINGS

WHAT YOU NEED

1½ cups frozen peaches
1 (5.3-ounce) container reduced-fat peach Greek yogurt
½ cup crushed ice
¼ teaspoon ground cinnamon
¾ cup reduced-fat milk or unsweetened almond milk
1-2 teaspoons honey (optional)

HOW TO MAKE IT

1 In a blender, place peaches, yogurt, ice and cinnamon. Pour in milk. If you like, add honey.
2 Cover and blend by turning blender on and off several times until the mixture is smooth.
3 Pour smoothie into glasses and serve.

Blueberry Oat Smoothie

MAKES 2 SERVINGS

WHAT YOU NEED

1½ cups frozen banana slices (see tip, page 31)
1½ cups frozen blueberries
¼ cup quick-cooking rolled oats
¼ cup almond butter
2 tablespoons ground flaxseeds
1½ cups to 2 cups unsweetened almond milk
1-2 teaspoons agave nectar (optional)

HOW TO MAKE IT

1 In a blender, place banana slices, blueberries, oats, almond butter and flaxseed. Pour in almond milk. If you like, add agave nectar.
2 Cover and blend by turning blender on and off several times until the mixture is smooth.
3 Pour smoothie into glasses and serve.

Rocking Raspberry Smoothie

MAKES 1 SERVING

WHAT YOU NEED

⅔ cup frozen banana slices (see tip, page 31)
⅔ cup frozen raspberries
1 (5.3-ounce) container reduced-fat raspberry yogurt
⅓ cup reduced-fat milk or unsweetened almond milk
1 teaspoon honey (optional)

HOW TO MAKE IT

1 In a blender, place banana slices, raspberries and yogurt. Pour in milk. If you like, add honey.
2 Cover and blend by turning blender on and off several times until the mixture is smooth.
3 Pour smoothie into glass and serve.

Fruity Avocado Spinach Green Smoothie

MAKES 2 SERVINGS

WHAT YOU NEED

½ cup frozen banana slices (see tip, page 31)
1 cup frozen mango chunks
1 cup baby spinach
½ cup chopped avocado
1 cup unsweetened almond milk or another dairy-free milk
½ teaspoon vanilla extract
1-2 teaspoons honey (optional)

HOW TO MAKE IT

1 In a blender, place banana slices, mango chunks, spinach and avocado. Pour in milk and vanilla. If you like, add honey.
2 Cover and blend by turning blender on and off several times until the mixture is smooth.
3 Pour smoothie into glasses and serve.

Smoothie Bingo

Create Your Own Recipe Play recipe bingo and see what combos you can come up with for your own tasty smoothies! To start, first make mini bingo cards with 3 boxes across and 3 boxes down (see illustration at left). The middle box is free (draw in a blender). Then have each player create their own bingo card by either drawing or writing in their favorite smoothie ingredients. (See suggestions below.) For the first column, draw or write in fruits or vegetables, for the second column draw power boosts, and for the third column draw your favorite juices and dairy or nondairy products. Instead of using bingo balls, on small pieces of paper write each of the ingredients that are on anyone's bingo cards.

To Play the Game Fold the pieces of paper and put them in a bowl. Pull the pieces of paper out of the bowl one by one and mark an "X" on your card if an ingredient on your card is called. The first player to X out a row horizontally or diagonally wins. Use the winning bingo ingredients for your next smoothie!

COLUMN 1 (Y) **Fresh or Frozen Fruit or Veggie (1 cup)**	COLUMN 2 (U) **Power Boost (use 1 to 2 tablespoons)**	COLUMN 3 (M) **Liquid Base (use 1 cup)**
• Bananas • Berries • Mangoes • Melons • Peaches • Avocados • Kale • Spinach • Arugula	• Nuts • Peanut butter • Almond butter • Chia seeds • Goji berries • Oats	• Dairy milk • Rice, almond or soy milk • Nonfat Greek yogurt • 100% fruit juice

BLENDER SAFETY

Always let a grown-up know when you plan to make a smoothie.

Have a grown-up show you how to use the blender safely. Never use a blender or sharp knives without permission.

Always have the lid securely on the blender container before turning on the blender. You may want to hold the lid down while the blender is running.

Never insert a spoon or anything else into the blender while it is running. Always turn off the blender before you stir the mixture.

Ask a grown-up to wash the sharp blades inside the blender after you're done making your smoothie.

PREP TIP

Freezing Bananas

Keep frozen chunks of bananas on hand so you can whip up smoothies at a moment's notice.

☐ To freeze bananas, unpeel and cut them into ½- to 1-inch slices.

☐ To keep bananas from turning brown, put slices into a small bowl. Pour about 2 to 3 tablespoons orange juice over bananas. Toss with a spoon until slices are coated with juice.

☐ Drain the banana slices and put them into a resealable plastic bag.

☐ Seal the bag. Place the bag on a tray and spread out the bananas in a single layer in the bag.

☐ Place the tray and bag in the freezer. When banana slices are frozen solid, remove the tray from the freezer and store the bag in the freezer.

☐ To use, remove frozen banana slices and place them in a blender with other smoothie ingredients (1 medium banana = ½ to ⅔ cup slices).

35

A-B-C Chicken
Noodle Soup

chapter 2

KID-APPROVED LUNCHES & SNACKS

EVEN THE FUSSIEST EATERS WILL GIVE A THUMBS-UP
TO THESE MIDDAY MEALS.

MIDDAY MEALS

GO BEYOND PB&J FOR FUN LUNCHTIME OPTIONS THAT
ARE SURE TO PLEASE KIDS OF ALL AGES.

⬇
tools

Measuring cups • Measuring spoons • 2 sharp knives* • 2 cutting boards* • Large saucepan • Wooden spoon • Ladle

*Use separate knives and cutting boards for poultry and vegetables.

💙

A-B-C Chicken Noodle Soup

MAKES 6 SERVINGS

WHAT YOU NEED

- 2 teaspoons vegetable oil
- 1 large yellow onion, chopped
- 2 celery ribs, diced
- 1 carrot, diced
- 1 (32-ounce) container chicken broth
- 2 cups water
- ½ teaspoon dried thyme leaves
- ½ teaspoon salt
- ¼ teaspoon ground black pepper
- 6 small boneless, skinless chicken breasts, diced
- ½ cup dried alphabet or tiny shell pasta or orzo
- 2 tablespoons finely chopped fresh parsley

HOW TO MAKE IT

1 In a large saucepan over medium heat, heat oil. Add onion, celery and carrot. Use a wooden spoon to stir as you cook until onion begins to soften, about 3 minutes.
2 Carefully pour in broth and water. Add thyme, salt and pepper. Bring to boil. Add chicken and pasta.
3 Reduce heat. Cover and simmer 10 minutes or until chicken is completely cooked through and pasta is tender, stirring occasionally with a wooden spoon.
4 Stir in parsley. Ladle soup into bowls.

Corn Dog Mini Muffins

MAKES 48 MUFFINS

WHAT YOU NEED

        Nonstick cooking spray
  1   cup all-purpose flour
  1   cup yellow cornmeal
  ½   cup white sugar
  ½   teaspoon baking soda
  ½   teaspoon salt
  2   eggs
  1   cup buttermilk
  1   stick (½ cup) butter, melted
8-10 all-beef hot dogs, cut into 1-inch bites

HOW TO MAKE IT

1 Preheat oven to 375 F. Lightly spray 48 (1¾-inch) cups of a mini muffin pan with nonstick spray. Set muffin pan aside.

2 In a large bowl, place flour, cornmeal, sugar, baking soda and salt. Use a wire whisk to stir until mixed.

3 In a medium bowl, place eggs, buttermilk and melted butter. Use a wire whisk to stir until mixed. Make a hole in center of flour mixture. Pour egg mixture into flour mixture. Use a wooden spoon to stir just until mixed (batter will be slightly lumpy).

4 Spoon about 1 tablespoon batter into each muffin cup. Place 1 hot dog piece in the middle of each cup.

5 Bake 8 to 12 minutes or until cornbread is golden brown.

6 Use hot pads to remove pan from oven. Place pan on a wire cooling rack. Cool muffins in muffin cups for 5 minutes. Use a table knife to loosen muffins from pan.

7 To store leftovers, make sure muffins are completely cool before putting them in a container with a tight-fitting lid. Store in refrigerator up to 3 days. Before serving, reheat muffins in a microwave 20 to 30 seconds.

⇩ **tools**

Measuring cups • Measuring spoons • Table knife • Cutting board • Mini muffin pan • Large bowl • Wire whisk • Medium bowl • Wooden spoon • Hot pads • Wire cooling rack

tools

Measuring cups •
Measuring spoons • Sharp
knife • Cutting board •
Large saucepan •
Colander • Large bowl •
Wooden spoon •
Plastic wrap

Dress up this salad
with bow ties!

Creamy Ranch and BLT Pasta Salad

MAKES 8 SERVINGS

WHAT YOU NEED

8	ounces dried bow tie pasta (farfalle)
½	cup mayonnaise
½	cup sour cream or plain Greek yogurt
2	tablespoons dry ranch dressing mix
2	tablespoons white vinegar
1½	cups grape tomatoes, cut in half
1	cup cubed provolone cheese
8	slices bacon, crisp-cooked and crumbled
¼	cup chopped red onion
1½	cups finely chopped romaine lettuce
	Salt and ground black pepper

HOW TO MAKE IT

1 In a large saucepan of boiling water, cook pasta according to package directions. Drain in colander. Rinse under cold water and drain again.

2 In a large bowl, use a wooden spoon to stir together mayonnaise, sour cream, ranch dressing mix and vinegar until mixed.

3 Stir cooled pasta into mayonnaise mixture. Stir in tomatoes, cheese, bacon and red onion. Gently stir in lettuce. Season to taste with salt and pepper.

4 Cover with plastic wrap and refrigerate at least 1 hour before serving.

Spaghetti Rings and Meatballs

MAKES 6 TO 8 SERVINGS

WHAT YOU NEED

- 2½ cups canned tomato sauce
- 1½ cups water
- 1 teaspoon garlic powder
- ½ teaspoon salt
- ⅛ teaspoon ground black pepper
- 6 ounces dried, ring-shape pasta
- 8 ounces frozen cooked mini meatballs, thawed
- ½ stick (¼ cup) butter
- ¼ cup milk
- ½ cup shredded mild cheddar cheese

HOW TO MAKE IT

1 In a large saucepan, use a wooden spoon to stir together tomato sauce, water, garlic powder, salt and pepper until mixed.

2 Over high heat, bring mixture to boil. Add pasta; stir to mix. Reduce heat to medium. Cover and cook 15 minutes or until pasta is tender, stirring often.

3 Add meatballs to saucepan. Stir until meatballs are coated. Cook until heated through.

4 Remove saucepan from stove. Stir in butter and milk.

5 Spoon spaghetti and meatballs into serving bowls. Sprinkle with cheese and serve.

tools
- Measuring cups
- Measuring spoons
- Can opener
- Large saucepan
- Wooden spoon

Better than the canned stuff!

⬇

tools

Measuring cups •
Measuring spoons •
Sharp knife • Cutting board •
Baking sheet • Foil • Medium
bowl • Wooden spoon • Rolling
pin • Ruler • Pizza cutter •
Pastry brush • Fork •
Hot pads • Pancake
turner

Little biscuit
pillows
stuffed with
goodness!

Cheesy Ham Broccoli Turnovers

MAKES 9 TURNOVERS

WHAT YOU NEED

Nonstick cooking spray

1¼ cups chopped fully cooked honey ham slices

1 cup chopped fresh broccoli

¾ cup shredded Italian cheese blend

All-purpose flour

1 (10-ounce) container refrigerated pizza dough

1 tablespoon milk

HOW TO MAKE IT

1 Preheat oven to 400 F. Cover a baking sheet with foil. Lightly spray foil with nonstick spray. Set baking sheet aside.

2 For filling, in a medium bowl, use a wooden spoon to stir together ham, broccoli and cheese until well mixed.

3 Lightly sprinkle a large clean cutting board with flour. Unroll pizza dough onto floured surface. Use a rolling pin to roll dough into a 12-inch square. Use a pizza cutter to cut dough into nine 4-inch squares.

4 Spoon about ⅓ cup filling onto the center of each square. Use a pastry brush dipped in water to moisten edges of dough. Fold dough in half over filling. Use fork to press edges of dough to seal. Use fork to poke holes in top of each turnover. Place turnovers on baking sheet.

5 Use a pastry brush to brush tops of turnovers with milk. Bake 13 to 15 minutes or until lightly golden. Use a pancake turner to remove turnovers from baking sheet and place on plates. Serve warm.

Pear Grilled Cheese Sandwiches

MAKES 4 SERVINGS

WHAT YOU NEED

Nonstick cooking spray

8 slices cinnamon-raisin bread

8 slices Muenster cheese

1 large pear, cored and thinly sliced

¼ cup dried cherries or cranberries

tools

Measuring cups • Apple corer • Sharp knife • Cutting board • Nonstick skillet or panini pan • Pancake turner

HOW TO MAKE IT

1 Lightly spray a nonstick skillet or panini pan with nonstick spray. Put skillet or pan on stovetop over medium heat.

2 On a flat work surface, place 4 slices of bread. Top each with 2 slices of cheese. Place pear slices on top of the cheese. Sprinkle with cherries.

3 Place remaining bread slices on top to enclose sandwiches. Carefully place sandwiches in hot skillet or panini pan. Use a pancake turner to press down lightly on sandwiches.

4 Cook 3 to 5 minutes or until bread is toasted on both sides and cheese is melted, using a pancake turner to flip halfway through cooking.

5 Cut sandwiches in half and place on plates to serve.

Mac 'n' Cheese in a Mug

MAKES 1 SERVING

WHAT YOU NEED
- ½ cup dried elbow macaroni
- ½ cup water
  Pinch of salt
- ¼ cup shredded mild cheddar cheese
- 3 tablespoons milk
  Pinch of ground black pepper

HOW TO MAKE IT

1 In a large, microwave-safe mug, place macaroni, water and salt. Use a spoon to stir until mixed.

2 Place cup in a microwave oven and microwave 2 to 3 minutes. Use hot pads to remove mug from microwave; stir.

3 Add cheese, milk and pepper to macaroni in the mug. Use a spoon to stir until mixed. Microwave 30 seconds or until macaroni is tender. If necessary, let cool 1 to 2 minutes before eating.

⬇

tools

Measuring cups •
Measuring spoons •
Large microwave-safe
mug • Spoon •
Hot pads

BACK-TO-SCHOOL
LUNCH BOX
MAKEOVERS

THEY'LL LOOK FORWARD TO MIDDAY MEALTIME
WHEN THEY KNOW YOU'VE PACKED
YUMMY (AND HEALTHY) FOOD!

HEY KIDS!

Help pick out what you want to eat the night before.

Not-Boring Classic Box Lunch

☐ Ham, cheddar & apple sandwich: sliced ham, cheddar cheese and thinly sliced apple on whole-grain bread with honey mustard and mayonnaise

☐ Quick "trees and raisins": small broccoli florets, raisins, sunflower seeds and bacon tossed with creamy poppyseed or coleslaw dressing

☐ Whole-grain chocolate chip-oatmeal cookie

Farmers Market Spaghetti & Meatballs

☐ Cooked, whole-grain spaghetti tossed with jarred marinara and topped with premade turkey meatballs

☐ Mix of sugar snap peas and baby carrots with yogurt-based ranch dip

☐ Fresh strawberries

A bento box keeps everything in the right place!

Nuts are a great-tasting snack that's also highly nutritious!

Nibbles & Sips

☐ Hummus and turkey pinwheels: whole-wheat tortilla spread with hummus and topped with a halved slice of cheddar or Colby-Jack cheese, slices of turkey breast and sliced baby spinach, rolled up and cut into pinwheels

☐ Bottled all-vegetable and fruit smoothie or juice

☐ Small container of almonds or pistachios

Pack a small spoon or fork to help keep fingers clean.

Build-Your-Own Tacos

☐ Two taco-size whole-wheat tortillas

☐ Mix of shredded cooked chicken breast, black beans and corn

☐ Mix of shredded lettuce and halved grape tomatoes

☐ Purchased guacamole

☐ Finely shredded Mexican cheese blend

Soup, Salad & Stackers

☐ Soup of choice

☐ Rolled ham, squares of cheese, whole-grain wheat crackers and slices of cucumber and sweet pepper strips for stacking

☐ Fruit salad: Clementine segments, fresh strawberries and blueberries drizzled with thinned vanilla yogurt and sprinkled with granola

Kebabs & Crunchies

☐ Sandwich kebabs: small squares of bread, folded roast beef, grape tomatoes and cubes of cheese on small skewers

☐ Mix of beet and sweet potato chips

☐ "Ants on a log" made with celery sticks, almond butter and dried cranberries or cherries

A mix of sweet and savory makes taste buds happy.

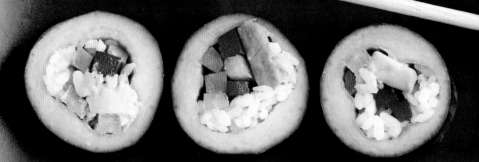

KIDS' SUSHI

HERE'S A GROWN-UP STYLE FOOD THAT YOUR LITTLE ONES WILL LOVE AND CAN EAT WITH THEIR FINGERS—FISH-FREE SUSHI!

tools

Sharp knife •
Cutting board •
Apple corer •
Small spoon
or knife

Cucumber Sushi Rolls

MAKES 2 SERVINGS

WHAT YOU NEED

- **2 medium cucumbers**
- **1 cup cooked and cooled long-grain white rice or Sushi Rice (see recipe, page 48)**
- **¼ cup thinly sliced avocado**
- **¼ cup thinly sliced red bell pepper**
- **¼ cup thinly sliced yellow bell pepper**
- **¼ cup thinly sliced carrot**
-   **Reduced-fat ranch dressing**

HOW TO MAKE IT

1 Cut each cucumber crosswise in half. Using an apple corer, small spoon or knife, remove seeds to create a long, hollow tube.

2 On a cutting board, place tubes on their sides. Spoon a small amount of rice into each tube, then press the rice toward one long side of each tube.

3 Carefully insert and place pieces of avocado, bell peppers and carrot on top of rice in tubes. Tubes should be nearly full. If any space remains, add more rice on top of vegetables, compressing and adding more rice until packed full.

4 With a sharp knife, slice cucumbers into 1-inch pieces. After slicing, stuff in additional rice and bell peppers where needed.

5 Place slices cut side down on plates or a platter. Serve with ranch dressing.

Sandwich Sushi

MAKES 4 SERVINGS

WHAT YOU NEED

- 4 slices whole-wheat or white bread
- ½ cup whipped cream cheese
- ¼ cup matchstick-cut or coarsely shredded carrot
- 2 tablespoons finely chopped red bell pepper
- 2 tablespoons finely chopped yellow bell pepper
- ¼ cup finely chopped cucumber
- ¼ cup finely chopped avocado
- Salt and ground black pepper

HOW TO MAKE IT

1 Cut crusts off bread slices.

2 Using a rolling pin, roll each bread slice to ⅛-inch thick. Spread 2 tablespoons cream cheese on each bread slice.

3 At the bottom of each bread slice, in a row, place some carrot, red and yellow bell peppers, cucumber and avocado. Use all the vegetables, evenly divided between slices. Lightly sprinkle with salt and pepper. Roll up slices into logs.

4 Place sandwich logs on a cutting board, seam side down. Gently cut each log into four pieces.

5 Arrange on plates or a serving platter to serve.

Use different colors of veggies for pretty fillings.

tools

Table knife •
Rolling pin •
Measuring spoons •
Cutting board

Veggie Sushi

MAKES 4 SERVINGS

WHAT YOU NEED

	Sushi Rice (see recipe, below right)
½	avocado, thinly sliced
1-2	teaspoons lemon juice
¼-⅓	cup toasted and/or black sesame seeds
4	sheets nori (edible seaweed)
½	English cucumber, seeded and cut into matchsticks
½	green, red and/or yellow bell pepper, cut into matchsticks

HOW TO MAKE IT

1 Prepare and cool Sushi Rice as directed. Sprinkle avocado slices with lemon juice.

2 To assemble sushi, on a bamboo sushi mat, sprinkle a thin layer of sesame seeds. Top with about ½ cup cooled rice in an even layer. Place a nori sheet on top. Then place one-fourth of the avocado, cucumber and bell pepper in a row down the middle of the rice.

3 Pick up the edge of the sushi mat. Fold the bottom edge of the mat up, enclose filling and tightly roll the sushi into a thick cylinder. Once the sushi is rolled, wrap it in the mat and gently squeeze to tightly compact it. Repeat with remaining ingredients to make a total of 4 rolls.

4 Place rolls on cutting board. Cut each roll into six to eight pieces. Place, cut side down, on serving platter; cover with damp paper towels until serving time.

SUSHI RICE

1 In a medium saucepan over high heat, stir together 1½ cups uncooked short-grain white rice and 1½ cups water. Bring to a boil; reduce heat to very low. Cover and simmer 15 minutes or until water is absorbed. Remove from heat. Let stand, covered, 10 minutes.

2 Meanwhile, in a small bowl, stir together ⅓ cup rice vinegar, 1 tablespoon sugar and 1 teaspoon salt; let stand until sugar is dissolved.

3 Fluff rice with a fork; transfer to a large bowl. Drizzle rice with vinegar mixture; toss until coated.

4 Cover work surface with a large piece of parchment. Spread rice over parchment; let cool. When cool, lightly cover with damp paper towels while preparing sushi.

⬇
tools

Sharp knife • Sushi mat •
Cutting board •
Medium saucepan •
Measuring cups •
Measuring spoons •
Large bowl •
Small bowl

Dessert Fruit Sushi

MAKES 6 TO 8 SERVINGS

WHAT YOU NEED

- 3 ounces (6 tablespoons) reduced-fat cream cheese, softened
- 3 tablespoons powdered sugar
- 1 teaspoon vanilla extract
- 3 (6-inch) flour tortillas or ready-made French crepes
- 1 small mango, finely chopped
- 1 small peach, finely chopped
- 1 small red apple, finely chopped
- 1 small kiwi, finely chopped

tools

Small bowl • Tablespoon or wooden spoon • Table knife • Cutting board • Sharp knife

HOW TO MAKE IT

1 In a small bowl, use a spoon to stir together cream cheese, powdered sugar and vanilla until well mixed.

2 Spread an equal amount of cream cheese mixture on each tortilla.

3 At the bottom of each tortilla, in a row, place some mango, peach, apple and kiwi. Use all the fruit, divided evenly between the tortillas. Roll up tightly, starting at the side with the fruit, to make a log shape.

4 Place tortilla logs on a cutting board, seam side down. Use a sharp knife to gently cut each log into 1-inch pieces.

5 Place, cut side down, on plates or a serving platter.

Serve with a drizzle of chocolate or fruit syrup.

A sweet & salty mix!

SMART SNACKS

MAKE BETWEEN-MEAL MUNCHING A HEALTHY AFFAIR FOR KIDS AND GROWN-UPS ALIKE WITH THESE GOOD-FOR-YOU SMALL BITES AND NIBBLES.

Happy Trails Mix

MAKES 6½ CUPS

WHAT YOU NEED

- 2   cups pretzel sticks
- 1   cup puffed corn cereal
- 1   cup honey-roasted peanuts
- 1   cup raisins or dried cranberries
- 1   cup mini marshmallows
- ½   cup M&M's candy or chocolate chips

HOW TO MAKE IT

1 In q large resealable plastic bag, place all ingredients. Seal bag; gently shake to mix.
2 Use a ½-cup measuring cup to portion out mix into snack-size resealable bags.

tools

Measuring cups •
1 large resealable
plastic bag • 13 snack-
size resealable
plastic bags

These smell so good baking in the oven!

Baked Soft Pretzels

MAKES 12 PRETZELS

tools

Measuring cups • Measuring spoons • 2 baking sheets • 2 small bowls • Spoon • Fork • Cutting board • Table knife • Ruler • Clean dish towel • Pastry brush • Hot pads • Pancake turner • Wire cooling rack • Medium bowl • Wooden spoon

WHAT YOU NEED

Nonstick cooking spray
1 cup hot water
2 teaspoons baking soda
1 egg
1 teaspoon cold water
3 1-pound frozen white bread dough loaves, thawed
All-purpose flour
Coarse kosher salt
Honey-Mustard Dip (see recipe, below right)

HOW TO MAKE IT

1 Generously spray two baking sheets with cooking spray. Set aside.
2 In a small bowl, stir together hot water and baking soda until baking soda is dissolved. Set aside.
3 In another small bowl, use a fork to beat egg and cold water. Set aside.
4 Using a table knife, cut each bread loaf into four pieces, making a total of 12 pieces. Lightly sprinkle a cutting board with flour. Roll each dough piece into a 36-inch long rope. (Keep unused dough covered with a clean dish towel to prevent it from drying out.)
5 Form ropes into pretzel shapes. Place pretzels about 1½ inches apart on baking sheets.

Use a pastry brush to brush pretzels with baking soda mixture. Let dough rise, uncovered, 30 minutes.
6 Preheat oven to 450 F. Use a pastry brush to brush pretzels with egg mixture. Lightly sprinkle pretzels with kosher salt.
7 Bake 12 to 15 minutes per batch or until lightly browned. Use a pancake turner to place pretzels on a wire cooling rack. Let cool slightly. Serve warm with Honey-Mustard Dip.

HONEY-MUSTARD DIP

In a medium bowl, use a wooden spoon to stir together ½ cup mayonnaise, 3 tablespoons honey, 2 tablespoons yellow mustard, 1 tablespoon Dijon mustard and 1½ teaspoons fresh lemon juice until mixed.

CINNAMON-SUGAR BAKED SOFT PRETZELS

Make pretzels as directed, except omit kosher salt and Honey-Mustard Dip. In a small bowl, use a spoon to stir together ¼ cup white sugar and 1 teaspoon ground cinnamon. Sprinkle on pretzels before baking.

Black Bean and Cheese Nachos

MAKES 4 SERVINGS

WHAT YOU NEED

- 1 cup refried black beans
- ½ cup salsa
- 4 cups tortilla chips (4 ounces)
- 1 cup shredded Mexican cheese blend
- ¼ cup each: chopped onions, chopped tomatoes, sliced black olives and guacamole
- ¼ cup sliced jalapeños (optional)

HOW TO MAKE IT

1 In a medium bowl, use a wooden spoon to stir together beans and salsa until mixed.

2 Spread chips onto a large, microwave-safe plate. Using a tableware teaspoon, spoon bean mixture on top of chips in small spoonfuls. Sprinkle with cheese.

3 Microwave 2 to 3 minutes or until cheese is melted. Top with onions, tomatoes, olives, guacamole and, if you like, jalapeños.

tools

Measuring cups • Can opener • Sharp knife • Cutting board • Medium bowl • Wooden spoon • Large, microwave-safe plate • Tableware teaspoon

53

Swap the crunch of a potato chip for the crunch of a radish!

⬇
tools

Measuring cups • Measuring spoons • Can opener • Citrus squeezer • Sharp knife • Cutting board • Wire strainer • Medium bowl • Food processor • Spoon • Serving bowl

Peanut Butter Hummus

MAKES 4 SERVINGS

WHAT YOU NEED

- 1 (15.5-ounce) can chickpeas, drained
- 2 tablespoons fresh lemon juice
- 2 tablespoons creamy peanut butter
- ½ teaspoon chopped garlic
- 2 tablespoons olive oil
  Salt and ground black pepper
- ¼ cup chopped peanuts (optional)
- ⅛ teaspoon paprika (optional)
  Assorted fresh vegetable slices and/or multigrain pita chips

HOW TO MAKE IT

1 Put a wire strainer over a medium bowl. Pour chickpeas into strainer to drain. Rinse chickpeas under cold running water and let drain again.

2 In the container of a food processor, add chickpeas, lemon juice, peanut butter and garlic. Cover and process until nearly smooth. With processor running, slowly pour in olive oil. If necessary, add water by the tablespoon until dip is a consistency you like. Season to taste with salt and pepper.

3 Spoon hummus into a serving bowl. If you like, sprinkle with chopped peanuts and/or paprika. Serve with assorted vegetables and/or pita chips.

Baked Cauliflower Tots

MAKES 6 TO 8 SERVINGS

WHAT YOU NEED

- 2 cups cauliflower florets
- 3 tablespoons water
- Nonstick cooking spray
- 2 eggs
- 1 egg white
- ½ cup finely chopped white onion
- ½ cup Italian-seasoned panko breadcrumbs
- ½ cup finely shredded sharp cheddar cheese
- 3 tablespoons finely chopped fresh parsley
- Salt and ground black pepper
- Marinara sauce

HOW TO MAKE IT

1 In a pie plate, spread cauliflower; drizzle with water. Cover with a paper towel. Microwave 1 minute. Use a spoon to stir cauliflower; cover again. Microwave 1 to 2 minutes or until cauliflower is tender but not mushy.

2 Drain cauliflower in a colander. Spread cauliflower on a cutting board. Pat dry with paper towels. Use a sharp knife to finely chop cauliflower.

3 Preheat oven to 400 F. Spray a nonstick baking sheet with nonstick spray. Set aside.

4 In a medium bowl, use a wire whisk to beat eggs and egg white until mixed. Add cauliflower, onion, breadcrumbs, cheese and parsley. Stir with a wooden spoon until mixed. Season to taste with salt and pepper.

5 Roll 1 tablespoon of mixture into oval-shaped ball for each tot. Place tots on baking sheet. Bake 8 minutes. Use a pancake turner to flip tots. Bake 8 to 10 minutes or until cooked through and golden.

6 Meanwhile, in a small saucepan over medium heat, heat marinara sauce until warm.

7 Use a pancake turner to remove tots from baking sheet and place on plates. Serve with warm marinara for dipping.

tools

Measuring cups • Measuring spoons • Egg separator • Sharp knife • Cutting board • Glass pie plate • Paper towels • Colander • Nonstick baking sheet • Medium bowl • Wire whisk • Wooden spoon • Pancake turner • Small saucepan

Snacks on a stick.

tools

Measuring spoons •
Sharp knife • Cutting
board • Small
bowl • Spoon

Fruit 'n' Cheese Kebabs With Cinnamon Yogurt Dip

MAKES 4 SERVINGS

WHAT YOU NEED

- 1 8-ounce container plain Greek yogurt
- 2 tablespoons honey
- ¼ teaspoon ground cinnamon
- 8 fresh whole strawberries
- 8 chunks fresh or canned pineapple
- 8 chunks cantaloupe
- 8 cubes Monterey Jack or mild cheddar cheese
- 8 wooden or paper lollipop sticks, or skewers

HOW TO MAKE IT

1 To make dip, in a small bowl, stir together yogurt, honey and cinnamon until combined. Set aside.
2 On lollipop sticks or wooden skewers, alternately thread fruit and cheese. Serve kebabs with dip.

Starry Peanut Butter Sandwich Fruit Kebabs

MAKES 1 OR 2 SERVINGS

WHAT YOU NEED

- 3 slices white or whole-wheat bread
- 1 tablespoon creamy peanut butter
- 1 tablespoon strawberry jam or preserves
- 2-3 large strawberries, halved
- 4-6 seedless green grapes
   Wooden or paper lollipop or cake-pop sticks

HOW TO MAKE IT

1 Use a 1½-inch to 2-inch star or other cookie-cutter shapes to cut 10 to 12 shapes from bread (making matching pairs).

2 Use a table knife to spread peanut butter on half of the bread shapes. Spread jam on remaining shapes. Press together to make five or six small sandwiches.

3 On lollipop or cake-pop sticks, alternately thread sandwiches, strawberry halves and grapes. Serve immediately.

⬇

tools

Measuring spoons •
Sharp knife • Cutting board •
1½- to 2-inch star-shaped
(or other shape) cookie
cutter • Table knife
or small narrow
spatula

Mix and match the
shapes and fruits.

Create a garden of veggies to share or a mini garden just for you.

tools

Measuring cups • Measuring spoons • Can opener • Strainer • Food processor • Medium bowl • Sharp knife • Cutting board • Small spatula • 6 shallow individual dishes or 9x5-inch baking dish

Black Bean Dip Garden

MAKES 6 SERVINGS

WHAT YOU NEED

- 2 (15-ounce) cans black beans
- ⅓ cup chopped white onion
- 2 tablespoons minced cilantro
- 2 tablespoons fresh lime juice
- 1 clove garlic, peeled and chopped
- 2 tablespoons minced jalapeño
- ¼ teaspoon ground cumin
- ¼ teaspoon chili powder
- ¼ teaspoon salt
  Assorted vegetables: baby carrots, zucchini, radishes, sweet peppers; tiny broccoli and/or cauliflower florets and/or asparagus tops

HOW TO MAKE IT

1 To make dip, put a wire strainer over a medium bowl. Pour beans into strainer to drain. Rinse beans under cold running water and let drain again.

2 In the container of a food processor, add beans, onion, cilantro, lime juice, garlic, jalapeño, cumin, chili powder and salt. Cover and process until mixture is smooth.

3 In shallow individual dishes or a 9x5-inch baking dish, use a spatula to spread dip to make garden "soil."

4 "Plant" assorted vegetables in dip so they look like they're growing in a garden.

COOL DRINKS

FROM PRETTY PINK AND ROSY RED TO
YELLOW-ORANGE, THESE REFRESHING FRUIT DRINKS
WILL WET YOUR WHISTLE.

Fizzy Strawberry Soda

MAKES 2 SERVINGS

WHAT YOU NEED
1 cup fresh or frozen strawberries
1 cup reduced-fat vanilla frozen yogurt
1 cup reduced-fat milk
1 cup sparkling water, divided

HOW TO MAKE IT
1 In a blender, place strawberries, frozen yogurt and milk.
2 Cover and blend by turning blender on and off several times until the mixture is smooth.
3 Pour mixture into glasses. Pour ½ cup sparkling water on top of each.

tools
Measuring cups •
Ice cream scoop •
Blender

Get fancy and add a mint leaf garnish.

Creamy Juice Punch

MAKES 2 SERVINGS

WHAT YOU NEED

- 1 (6-ounce) container frozen orange, grape, pineapple or fruit punch juice concentrate*
- 1 cup water
- 1 cup whole milk
- ¼ cup white sugar
- 2 teaspoons vanilla extract
- 1 cup ice cubes
- 4 orange slices or pineapple chunks (optional)

HOW TO MAKE IT

1 In a blender, place frozen juice concentrate, water, milk, sugar, vanilla and ice cubes.

2 Cover and blend by turning blender on and off several times until the mixture is smooth.

3 Pour mixture into glasses. If you like, garnish glasses with orange slices or pineapple chunks.

✱ If you can't find 6-ounce containers of frozen juice concentrate at your grocery store, purchase a 12-ounce container and use only half of it. Cover and freeze the remaining half for use at another time.

tools

Measuring cups
Measuring spoons
Sharp knife
Cutting board
Blender

Sparkling Watermelon Spritzer

MAKES 2 SERVINGS

WHAT YOU NEED

- 1 cup cubed seedless watermelon
- 1 cup sparkling white grape juice
- 1 tablespoon grenadine or pomegranate syrup
- Ice cubes
- 2 melon skewers* (optional)

HOW TO MAKE IT

1 In a blender, place watermelon, grape juice and grenadine. Cover and blend 20 to 30 seconds or until slushy.

2 Put a wire strainer over the top of a wide-mouth pitcher. Pour watermelon mixture into strainer. Discard fruit pulp remaining in strainer.

3 Put ice cubes in glasses. Pour mixture over ice. If you like, garnish each drink with a melon skewer.

✱ To make melon skewers, using a melon baller, scoop two balls each from a watermelon and a cantaloupe or honeydew melon. Thread one of each type of melon ball onto a skewer.

Most watermelon is red, but some types come in orange and yellow, too!

tools

Measuring cups •
Measuring spoons •
Sharp knife • Blender •
Cutting board •
Wire strainer • Pitcher •
Melon baller

Blushing Pink Lemonade

MAKES 2 SERVINGS

WHAT YOU NEED

- 1¼ cups white sugar
- 4 cups water, divided
- 1 cup unsweetened cranberry juice
- 1 cup fresh lemon juice
- Ice cubes
- Fresh mint leaves (optional)
- Lemon wedges (optional)

HOW TO MAKE IT

1 In a small saucepan over medium heat, add sugar and 1 cup water, stirring with a wooden spoon until sugar is completely dissolved. Remove pan from heat.

2 Pour remaining 3 cups water, cranberry juice and lemon juice into a large pitcher. Pour in warm sugar-water mixture. Refrigerate for at least 1 hour before serving.

3 Put ice cubes in glasses. Pour lemonade over ice. If you like, garnish each drink with mint leaves and lemon wedges.

tools

Measuring cups •
Sharp knife • Cutting
board • Citrus squeezer •
Small saucepan •
Wooden spoon •
Large pitcher

75
Sweet Potato
Tot Casserole

» » » chapter 3 « « «

FAMILY SUPPERS

TURN MEALTIME INTO AN OPPORTUNITY FOR BONDING, WITH
THESE DELICIOUS DINNERS YOU CAN MAKE TOGETHER.

Eat up! When the whole family gets involved, meals become more fun.

DINNER'S READY

GATHER THE WHOLE FAMILY AROUND FOR A DELICIOUS MEAL THAT'LL HAVE EVERYONE ASKING FOR SECONDS.

Spaghetti Pizza Casserole

MAKES 4 TO 6 SERVINGS

WHAT YOU NEED
For the crust

Nonstick cooking spray
8 ounces dried spaghetti
1 egg
⅓ cup whole milk
¼ teaspoon salt
¼ teaspoon garlic powder
1 cup shredded pizza-blend cheese

For the toppings

1½ cups marinara sauce
3 ounces sliced pepperoni (packaged)
1 cup shredded pizza-blend cheese

HOW TO MAKE IT

1 Preheat oven to 400 F. Lightly spray a 9-inch pie plate with nonstick spray. Set aside.
2 In a large saucepan, cook spaghetti according to package directions. Drain in a colander. Rinse under cold water; drain again. Put spaghetti in a large bowl; set aside.
3 In a small bowl, use a wire whisk to stir egg, milk, salt and garlic powder until well mixed.
4 Pour egg mixture over spaghetti. Add 1 cup pizza-blend cheese. Use a wooden spoon to stir until mixed. Pour spaghetti mixture into pie plate. Bake for 15 minutes.
5 Reduce oven temperature to 350 F. Pour marinara sauce over spaghetti. Top with pepperoni. Sprinkle with 1 cup pizza cheese.
6 Bake 20 to 25 minutes or until cheese is bubbly. Use hot pads to remove casserole from oven; let cool several minutes before serving.

⬇
tools
Measuring cups • Measuring spoons • 9-inch pie plate • Large saucepan • Colander • Large bowl • Small bowl • Wire whisk • Wooden spoon • Hot pads

Crispy Chicken Nuggets

MAKES 4 TO 6 SERVINGS

WHAT YOU NEED

- ¼ cup all-purpose flour
- 1 tablespoon cornstarch
- 2 teaspoons coarse kosher salt
- 1 teaspoon Italian seasoning
- ½ teaspoon paprika
- ¼ teaspoon ground black pepper
- ¼ teaspoon garlic powder
- ¼ teaspoon onion powder
- 1 egg white
- ½ cup buttermilk
- 2 cups plain panko breadcrumbs
- 4 tablespoons butter, melted
- 1½ pounds boneless, skinless chicken breasts, cut into 1½-inch pieces
  Barbecue sauce

HOW TO MAKE IT

1 In a shallow bowl or pie plate, use a fork to stir together flour, cornstarch, salt, Italian seasoning, paprika, black pepper, garlic powder and onion powder. In another shallow bowl, use a fork or wire whisk to beat egg white and buttermilk. In a third shallow bowl, toss breadcrumbs and butter until well mixed.

2 Place a wire rack inside a large rimmed baking sheet.

3 To coat chicken, using tongs, dip a chicken piece into flour mixture; shake off excess. Dip chicken into buttermilk mixture, then breadcrumb mixture (gently pat breadcrumb mixture onto chicken to adhere). Place on wire rack. Repeat with remaining chicken.

4 Let chicken stand at room temperature 10 minutes to let coating set.

5 Preheat oven to 375 F. Bake chicken on wire rack 15 to 20 minutes or until a thermometer inserted into the biggest chicken piece registers 165 F.

6 Use hot pads to remove pan from oven. Let chicken cool slightly before serving with barbecue sauce on the side.

tools

Measuring cups • Measuring spoons • Egg separator • Sharp knife • Cutting board • 3 shallow bowls or pie plates • Spoon • Small wire whisk or fork • Wire rack • Large rimmed baking sheet • Tongs • Instant-read thermometer • Hot pads

Savory Slow-Cooked Pork Chops

MAKES 4 SERVINGS

WHAT YOU NEED

- ½ cup all-purpose flour, divided
- ½ teaspoon garlic powder
- ½ teaspoon ground mustard
- ¼ teaspoon seasoned salt
- ¼ teaspoon ground black pepper
- 4 boneless pork loin chops (4 ounces each)
- 2 tablespoons vegetable oil
- 1 (14.5-ounce) can chicken or vegetable broth

HOW TO MAKE IT

1 In a large resealable plastic bag, place ¼ cup flour, garlic powder, mustard, seasoned salt and black pepper. Seal bag and shake to mix. Add pork chops, one at a time, and shake to coat. Place coated pork chops on a plate.

2 In a large skillet over medium-high heat, heat oil until shimmering. Add chops to skillet; brown on both sides, using tongs to flip each chop.

3 Remove chops from skillet and place in a 5-quart slow cooker. Pour broth over chops. Cover and cook on low 2 to 3 hours or until meat is tender.

4 Use tongs to remove pork chops from slow cooker; place on a serving platter. Cover chops with foil to keep warm.

5 Turn cooker heat to high. Using a wire whisk, stir remaining flour into cooking juices in slow cooker. Cover and cook on high, stirring occasionally, until gravy is slightly thick. Serve gravy over pork chops.

Carrot "coins" add color and nutrition!

⬇

tools

Measuring cups • Measuring spoons • Sharp knife • Cutting board • Large skillet • Tongs • Paper towels • Wooden spoon • Metal spoon • Large baking sheet • Small bowl • Pastry brush • Hot pads • Wire cooling rack

Loaded Cheeseburger Crescent Ring

MAKES 8 SERVINGS

WHAT YOU NEED

- 4 slices bacon
- 1 pound lean ground beef
- ¼ cup ketchup
- 2 tablespoons yellow mustard
- 2 tablespoons finely chopped onion
- 2 (8-ounce) containers refrigerated crescent dinner rolls
- 16 dill pickle slices (chips)
- 4 slices American cheese, cut in half
- 2 teaspoons sesame seeds

HOW TO MAKE IT

1 Preheat oven to 375 F. In a large cold skillet, place bacon in a single layer. Cook over medium heat 8 to 10 minutes. Use tongs to flip bacon. Cook another 4 to 6 minutes or until slightly crisp. Remove bacon from skillet and place on paper towels to drain. Drain bacon drippings (have a grown-up help with this step).

2 Place ground beef into skillet. Set heat to medium-high. Use a wooden spoon to stir beef to break up large chunks. When beef is cooked, remove skillet from heat. Push beef to one side of skillet.

3 Slightly lift and tip skillet so drippings flow from meat to opposite side of skillet. Using a metal spoon, scoop out drippings.

4 Spoon beef from skillet into a small bowl. Chop bacon and add it to ground beef. Use a wooden spoon to stir in ketchup, mustard and onion until mixed.

5 Open containers of crescent rolls. Separate the rolls into eight rectangles. On a large baking sheet, overlap and arrange rectangles in a ring. Short sides of rectangles should form a 5-inch circle in center.

6 Spoon beef mixture on the half of each rectangle closest to center/inside of ring; top each rectangle with 2 pickle slices and 1 piece of cheese.

7 Bring the dough rectangle from the outer side of the ring up and over filling. Tuck the top edge of dough under bottom layer of dough to secure it. Repeat around ring until entire filling is enclosed (some filling might show a little).

8 Gently pull apart dough perforations on the top until filling peeks through. Use a pastry brush to lightly brush dough with water. Sprinkle sesame seeds on top.

9 Bake 20 to 25 minutes or until dough is golden brown and filling is heated through. Use hot pads to remove baking sheet from oven and place it on a wire cooling rack. Let cool 5 to 10 minutes, then cut into pieces to serve.

Getting your (clean) hands dirty is just part of the cooking fun!

It's a burger that's stuffed instead of stacked.

Breaded Salmon Fish Sticks

MAKES 4 TO 6 SERVINGS

WHAT YOU NEED

For the fish sticks

Olive oil

1 (18-ounce) skinless, center-cut salmon fillet (about 9×4 inches and ½ inch thick)

½ cup all-purpose flour

½ teaspoon coarse kosher salt

¼ teaspoon ground black pepper

3 egg whites

1 cup grated Romano or Asiago cheese

1 cup Italian-seasoned panko breadcrumbs

For the dipping sauce

⅓ cup reduced-fat mayonnaise

⅓ cup reduced-fat plain Greek yogurt

1 tablespoon Dijon mustard

1 tablespoon chopped fresh parsley or chives

HOW TO MAKE IT

1 Preheat oven to 450 F. Using a pastry brush, generously spread olive oil on a large rimmed baking sheet. Set aside.

2 Rinse salmon fillet. Pat dry with paper towels. Cut fillet crosswise in half to make two pieces, each about 4½ x 4 inches. Starting from a long edge, cut each fish piece into ½-inch-wide strips.

3 In a shallow bowl or pie plate, use a spoon to stir together flour, salt and pepper. In another shallow bowl, use a fork or wire whisk to beat egg whites until frothy. In a third shallow bowl, use a spoon to stir together cheese and breadcrumbs.

4 To coat fish sticks, using tongs, dip a fish stick into flour mixture; shake off excess. Dip fish stick in egg whites, then cheese mixture (gently pat cheese mixture onto fish stick to adhere). Repeat with remaining fish sticks.

5 Place fish sticks on baking sheet. Lightly drizzle with olive oil.

6 Bake 15 to 20 minutes until golden brown, using tongs to flip sticks once halfway through baking.

7 Meanwhile, make dipping sauce. In a small bowl, use a spoon to stir together mayonnaise, yogurt, Dijon mustard and parsley.

8 Use hot pads to remove baking sheet from oven. Use tongs to place fish sticks on serving platter. Serve with dipping sauce on the side.

tools

Measuring cups • Measuring spoons • Ruler • Egg separator • Grater • Pastry brush • Large rimmed baking sheet • Sharp knife • Cutting board • Paper towels • 3 shallow bowls or pie plates • 2 Spoons • Small wire whisk or fork • Tongs • Small bowl • Hot pads

Super easy to make.

Sweet Potato Tot Casserole

MAKES 5 SERVINGS

WHAT YOU NEED

- 1 pound lean ground beef
- ½ cup chopped white onion
- 1 (10.75-ounce) can condensed cream of mushroom soup
- 1 tablespoon ketchup
- 1 tablespoon Worcestershire sauce
- 3 cups frozen sweet potato tots or veggie tots
  Chopped green scallions

HOW TO MAKE IT

1 Preheat oven to 425 F.

2 In a large skillet over medium-high heat, place ground beef and onion. Use a wooden spoon to stir beef to break up large chunks. Cook until beef is browned. Remove skillet from heat.

3 Push beef and onion mixture to one side of skillet. Slightly lift and tip skillet so drippings flow from mixture to opposite side of skillet (have a grown-up help with this step). Using a metal spoon, scoop out drippings.

4 Add soup, ketchup and Worcestershire sauce to skillet; use a wooden spoon to stir well to combine. Spoon beef mixture into a 2-quart shallow baking dish or 9-inch pie plate. Arrange tots on top.

5 Bake 25 minutes or until tots are golden brown. Use hot pads to remove dish from oven. Sprinkle with chopped scallions.

tools

Measuring cups • Measuring spoons • Sharp knife • Cutting board • Can opener • Large skillet • Wooden spoon • Metal spoon • 2-quart baking dish or 9-inch pie plate • Hot pads

Weeknight Mini Meatloaves

MAKES 10 MINI MEATLOAVES

WHAT YOU NEED

1	egg
¼	teaspoon garlic powder
¼	teaspoon salt
¼	teaspoon ground black pepper
½	teaspoon Worcestershire sauce
1¾	pounds lean ground beef
⅓	cup finely chopped sweet white onion
⅓	cup quick-cooking rolled oats
3	tablespoons barbecue sauce
¾	cup shredded cheddar cheese

⇩

tools

Measuring cups • Measuring spoons • Sharp knife • Cutting board • Muffin pan • Foil bake-cup liners • Large bowl • Wire whisk • 2 spoons • Hot pads • Paper towels • Fork or small silicone spatula

HOW TO MAKE IT

1 Preheat oven to 400 F. Line 10 (2½-inch) cups of a muffin pan with foil bake cups. Set aside.

2 In a large bowl, use a wire whisk to beat egg well. Stir in garlic powder, salt, pepper and Worcestershire sauce. Crumble ground beef into bowl on top of egg mixture. Add onion and oats. Gently mix with clean hands, taking care not to overwork the meat.

3 Spoon equal amounts of meat mixture into each lined muffin cup; use back of spoon to press down firmly. Make a ¼-inch-deep indentation in each meatloaf. Bake 20 minutes.

4 Use hot pads to remove pan from oven. Use paper towels to carefully blot drippings from meatloaves. Spoon about 1 teaspoon barbecue sauce into each meatloaf indentation. Sprinkle each meatloaf with cheddar cheese.

5 Return muffin pan to oven and bake 1 to 2 minutes or until cheese is bubbly.

6 Use hot pads to remove pan from oven. Use a fork to loosen and remove meatloaves from pan. Place on plates to serve.

Making extras means you'll have plenty of leftovers to enjoy.

Top with extra barbecue sauce and cheese.

Chicken Veggie Pot Pie

MAKES 4 TO 6 SERVINGS

WHAT YOU NEED

- 1 cup bite-size pieces of cooked chicken
- 1⅔ cups frozen mixed vegetables, thawed
- 1 (10.75-ounce) can condensed cream of chicken soup
- 1 egg
- ½ cup whole milk
- 1 cup all-purpose baking biscuit mix

HOW TO MAKE IT

1 Preheat oven to 400 F.

2 In a large bowl, use a wooden spoon to stir chicken, vegetables and soup until mixed. Spread mixture in a 2-quart baking dish or 9-inch pie plate. Set aside.

3 To make topping, in a medium bowl, use fork to beat egg well. Add milk and stir. Stir in baking mix; stir with fork just until mixed (batter will be slightly lumpy).

4 Pour topping over chicken mixture.

5 Bake 30 minutes or until top turns golden brown. Use hot pads to remove plate from oven.

tools

Measuring cups • Measuring spoons • Sharp knife • Cutting board • Can opener • Large skillet • Wooden spoon • Metal spoon • 2-quart baking dish or 9-inch pie plate • Hot pads

PASSPORT DINING

TRAVEL THE WORLD WITH THESE CROWD-PLEASING FOODS FROM AROUND THE GLOBE.

tools

13x9-inch baking dish •
Plastic wrap • Cutting
board • Meat mallet •
2 shallow bowls • Large
skillet • Measuring cups •
Measuring spoons •
Tongs • Hot pads

Italy

Cheesy Chicken Parmigiana

MAKES 4 SERVINGS

WHAT YOU NEED

- Nonstick cooking spray
- 4 boneless, skinless chicken breast halves
- 1 egg, slightly beaten
- ½ cup plain, fine breadcrumbs
- ½ cup grated Parmesan cheese
- 1 teaspoon Italian seasoning
- 2 tablespoons butter
- 1 (14-ounce) jar tomato-basil pasta sauce
- 1 cup shredded mozzarella cheese
- ½ cup shredded provolone cheese
- Fresh basil

HOW TO MAKE IT

1 Preheat oven to 375 F. Lightly spray a 13×9-inch baking dish with nonstick spray.

2 Place chicken between two sheets of plastic wrap. Place on cutting board. Using the flat side of a meat mallet, flatten to ½-inch thick.

3 In a shallow bowl or pie plate, place egg. In another shallow bowl, combine breadcrumbs, Parmesan cheese and Italian seasoning. Dip chicken into egg, then breadcrumb mixture.

4 In a large skillet over medium-high heat, melt butter. Add chicken; brown both sides, using tongs to turn meat. In prepared baking dish, place chicken in one layer.

5 Pour pasta sauce over chicken; sprinkle with mozzarella and provolone cheeses. Cover with foil. Bake 30 minutes or until chicken is cooked through and heated. Remove with hot pads. Garnish with basil to serve.

⬇
tools
Measuring cups •
Measuring spoons •
Large skillet • Wooden
spoon • Large spoon •
Sharp knife •
Cutting board •
Citrus squeezer

Thailand

Thai Chicken Lettuce Wraps

MAKES 6 SERVINGS

WHAT YOU NEED

1¼	pounds ground chicken or turkey
¼	cup chopped scallions
3	tablespoons chopped fresh cilantro
3	tablespoons creamy peanut butter
2	tablespoons fresh lime juice
1	tablespoon chopped fresh mint
1-2	teaspoons Sriracha sauce
1	teaspoon sugar
1	cup coarsely shredded carrots
⅓	cup chopped salted peanuts
6	medium Bibb lettuce leaves

HOW TO MAKE IT

1 In a large nonstick skillet over medium-high heat, cook chicken or turkey until cooked through, using a wooden spoon to stir it and break up large pieces. Drain and discard drippings.

2 Stir in scallions, cilantro, peanut butter, lime juice, mint, Sriracha and sugar. Lower heat to medium; cook 3 to 4 minutes until hot, stirring occasionally.

3 To serve, spoon 2 heaping tablespoons chicken mixture, 2 tablespoons carrots and 1 teaspoon peanuts onto center of each lettuce leaf; wrap around filling. Serve warm.

DINNERTIME AROUND THE WORLD

TURN MEALTIME INTO AN OPPORTUNITY TO LEARN ABOUT OTHER CULTURES WHILE ENJOYING FRESH FLAVORS AND INTERESTING CUISINE.

Take a monthly—or even a weekly—culinary trip with your family through the making of a meal from a different culture than yours. Food is a tasty tool for exploring the customs and traditions of other countries with your kids, as well as expanding their palates and increasing their awareness of diversity.

Work as a Team
Planning is half the fun! Choose a country or region for your global food journey together. Find a map, along with a picture of the country's flag, and research ingredients and foods associated with the locale. Use different country celebrations to teach kids about various types of foods, music and art. Depending on your child's age, they may also want to create a cultural photo collage, draw or color a picture, or learn about some basic facts to share with the rest of the family at the dinner table.

Find Mealtime Inspiration
Let the food be the star. Select kid-friendly recipes and meal accompaniments that represent the country. First choose a main dish, such as the Layered Beef Enchilada Casserole (p. 86), then complement it with a side of Mexican rice or refried beans, and frozen fruit pops or paletas for a healthy dessert. For an evening in Paris, serve Ham and Cheese Crepes (p. 87) with tossed greens dressed with a French vinaigrette, and colorful French macarons for dessert. Or take a trip to Italy with a salad, some Cheesy Chicken Parmigiana (p. 79) and some yummy gelato for dessert!

Further Cultural Food Explorations

☐ Visit ethnic grocery stores and bakeries.

☐ Shop at farmers markets for special produce used in different cuisines.

☐ Visit neighboring communities and dine at their local restaurants, or purchase ethnic foods from street food vendors.

☐ Read stories together or look at picture books to spark questions from kids about other cultures.

☐ Attend ethnic celebrations that are open to the public.

Dress the Table
Use table runners and napkins to show off the colors of a country. For example, for a Moroccan dinner, set the table using a fabric with jewel tones, such as ruby red, amethyst purple, sapphire blue and amber yellow. Decorate the table with bright flowers and a few votive candles placed in colorful glass holders. For an Italian night, choose a simple red-and-white checked tablecloth and adorn it with a rainbow candle in a vintage Chianti bottle along with a few silk grape leaves.

Look for Cultural Outfits
Kids love dressing up. Look online or in books for traditional dress and accessories of a country. Be sure your child understands that the clothing represents a culture, and that it is not a costume.

Invite Friends
If any of your family friends are of a different cultural background than yours, ask them to join you for dinner and share with your family information about their traditions, celebrations and important values. They may also want to bring a traditional family dish to share.

Turn on the Tunes
Play music from the region you're celebrating. Keep the volume low enough so that it doesn't interfere with conversations.

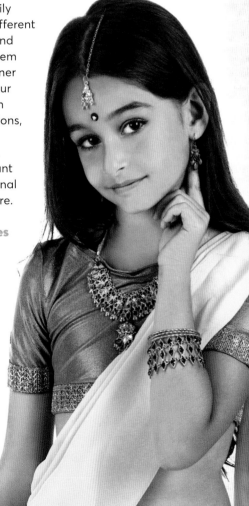

Indian Veggie Curry

MAKES 4 SERVINGS

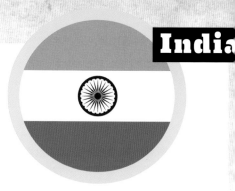
India

WHAT YOU NEED

1½ teaspoons canola oil
1 cup diced peeled sweet potato
1 cup small cauliflower florets
¼ cup thinly sliced white onion
2 teaspoons curry powder
1 (15.5-ounce) can chickpeas, drained and rinsed
1 (14.5-ounce) can diced tomatoes, undrained
½ cup vegetable broth
¼ teaspoon salt
Hot cooked basmati rice
Reduced-fat plain Greek yogurt
Fresh cilantro leaves

HOW TO MAKE IT

1 In a large nonstick skillet over medium-high heat, heat oil. Add sweet potato. Cook and stir 3 minutes. Reduce heat to medium. Add cauliflower, onion and curry powder. Cook and stir 1 minute.
2 Add chickpeas, undrained diced tomatoes, broth and salt. Bring to a boil; reduce heat. Cover and simmer 10 minutes or until vegetables are tender, stirring occasionally.
3 Divide rice among serving bowls. Top with curry, a spoon or two of yogurt and some cilantro leaves.

tools

Measuring cups •
Measuring spoons •
Large skillet • Serving
bowls • Can opener •
Strainer • Sharp knife •
Cutting board

tools

Measuring cups •
Measuring spoons •
Medium saucepan • Large
skillet • Can opener •
Strainer • Sharp knife •
Cutting board •
Serving bowl

Jamaica

Jamaican Coconut Rice and Red Beans

MAKES 6 TO 8 SERVINGS

WHAT YOU NEED

- 1 **cup long-grain white rice**
- 1¾ **cups water, divided**
- 1 **(13.5-ounce) can light coconut milk, divided**
- ¾ **teaspoon salt, divided**
- 1 **tablespoon coconut oil**
- 1 **large white onion, chopped**
- 1 **red bell pepper, chopped**
- 4 **cloves garlic, minced**
- ½ **teaspoon dried thyme leaves**
- ¼ **teaspoon ground allspice**
- ¼ **teaspoon ground cinnamon**
- ⅛ **teaspoon cayenne pepper (optional)**
- 1 **(15-ounce) can red kidney beans, drained and rinsed**

HOW TO MAKE IT

1 For coconut rice, in a medium saucepan over high heat, stir rice, 1¼ cups water, ¾ cup coconut milk and ¼ teaspoon salt. Bring to a boil; reduce heat to low. Cover; simmer 20 minutes or until liquid is absorbed.

2 Meanwhile, in a large, deep skillet over medium-high heat, heat coconut oil. Add onion, bell pepper and garlic; cook 10 minutes or until tender, stirring occasionally.

3 Stir in remaining salt, thyme, allspice, cinnamon and, if desired, cayenne. Cook and stir 1 minute.

4 Add beans, remaining coconut milk and remaining water. Bring to a simmer. Reduce heat to medium. Simmer 8 minutes or until thickened and heated, stirring occasionally. Remove from heat and stir in coconut rice; transfer to a serving bowl.

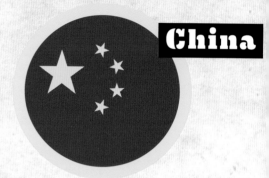

China

tools

Measuring cups •
Measuring spoons •
Colander • Cutting board •
Sharp knife • Medium
bowl • Small bowl •
Large skillet or wok •
Wooden spoon •
Serving bowl

DID YOU KNOW?

Chinese food varies
greatly by region:
Some dishes are
spicy with a lot of
seasonings, others
are sweet and light
or mostly sour.

Easy Beef Broccoli Lo Mein

MAKES 4 SERVINGS

WHAT YOU NEED

8 ounces dried lo mein noodles or spaghetti
8 ounces boneless beef sirloin or
  flat iron steak, cut ¼-inch thick
1 tablespoon cornstarch
3 tablespoons soy sauce, divided
¼ cup packed brown sugar
2 tablespoons hoisin sauce
½ teaspoon ground ginger
1 tablespoon vegetable oil
3 cups small broccoli florets
½ cup carrot matchsticks or thin red
  bell pepper strips
2 cloves garlic, minced
1 teaspoon Asian toasted sesame oil

HOW TO MAKE IT

1 Cook noodles according to package directions.
When cooked, drain in a colander. Set aside.
2 Meanwhile, cut steak into thin strips. In a medium
bowl, stir together cornstarch and 1 tablespoon soy
sauce. Add beef to bowl; marinate 5 to 10 minutes.
3 In a small bowl, combine remaining soy sauce,
brown sugar, hoisin sauce and ginger; set aside.
4 In a large skillet or wok over medium-high heat,
heat vegetable oil. Add beef; stir-fry 2 minutes or
until beef is no longer pink. Push beef toward edges
of skillet. Add broccoli, carrots or peppers, and
garlic to center of skillet. Stir-fry 5 minutes until
vegetables are crisp-tender.
5 Add cooked noodles and sauce to the beef-
vegetable mixture; drizzle with sesame oil. Toss to
combine. Transfer to a serving bowl and serve.

Moroccan Turkey Kebabs

MAKES 4 SERVINGS

WHAT YOU NEED

- ½ cup plain yogurt
- ⅓ cup chopped fresh parsley
- 3 tablespoons fresh lemon juice
- 1 tablespoon olive oil
- 3 cloves garlic, minced
- 2 teaspoons paprika
- 1 teaspoon ground cumin
- ½ teaspoon salt
- ¼ teaspoon ground black pepper
- 1 pound turkey tenderloins, trimmed and cut into 1-inch pieces
- 2 small red and/or yellow bell peppers, cut into 1½-inch pieces
- 1 medium zucchini, cut into ¼-inch-thick rounds

HOW TO MAKE IT

1 In a medium bowl, stir together yogurt, parsley, lemon juice, olive oil, garlic, paprika, cumin, salt and pepper. Transfer half of yogurt mixture to a small bowl; cover and refrigerate until serving.

2 Add turkey to remaining yogurt mixture. Cover and marinate in the refrigerator 20 minutes.

3 Preheat grill or broiler. Remove turkey from marinade; discard marinade. On skewers, alternately thread turkey, bell peppers and zucchini. Grill or broil kebabs 6 to 8 minutes or until the turkey is cooked through, turning kebabs halfway during grilling or broiling. Place on serving plates; serve with reserved yogurt mixture for a sauce.

tools

Measuring cups • Measuring spoons • Plastic wrap • Medium bowl • Small bowl • Wooden skewers • Sharp knife • Cutting board • Citrus squeezer • Grill or broiler pan • Serving plates

tools

Measuring cups • Measuring spoons • Wooden spoon • Large skillet • 13x9-inch baking dish • Sharp knife • Cutting board • Hot pads

Mexico

Layered Beef Enchilada Casserole

MAKES 6 SERVINGS

WHAT YOU NEED

- 1 **pound lean ground beef**
- ¾ **cup chopped yellow onion**
- 2 **cloves garlic, minced**
- 1 **(4.5-ounce) can diced green chiles**
- ½ **teaspoon salt**
- ⅛ **teaspoon ground black pepper**
- 2 **(10-ounce) cans red enchilada sauce, divided**
- 8 **(6-inch) flour or corn tortillas, divided**
- 1 **cup shredded Mexican cheese blend**
  Sour cream
  Salsa
  Sliced black olives

HOW TO MAKE IT

1 Preheat oven to 375 F. In a large nonstick skillet over medium-high heat, cook ground beef, onion and garlic until beef is browned, stirring frequently to break up beef. Drain; discard drippings.

2 Stir in chiles, salt and pepper. Remove from heat.

3 To assemble casserole, in an ungreased 13x9-inch baking dish, pour 1 can of enchilada sauce. Arrange 4 tortillas on top, overlapping slightly. Spoon beef mixture evenly over tortillas. Top with remaining 4 tortillas; pour remaining can of enchilada sauce on top. Sprinkle evenly with cheese.

4 Bake 20 to 25 minutes or until thoroughly heated. Serve with sour cream, salsa and black olives.

Ham and Cheese Crepes

MAKES 4 SERVINGS

WHAT YOU NEED

- 8 ready-made French crepes, divided
- 2 cups shredded Gruyère, Swiss or cheddar cheese, divided
- 8 thin slices Black Forest ham, divided
  Sour cream
  Chopped fresh chives or dill
  Coarse-ground black pepper (optional)

HOW TO MAKE IT

1 Preheat oven to 180 F. Heat a nonstick medium skillet over medium-low heat. When pan is hot, place 1 crepe in pan. Sprinkle with about ¼ cup cheese. Place 1 slice ham on half of crepe. When cheese begins to melt, fold the side without ham up and over ham, forming a half-circle. Then fold in half again, making a quarter-circle.

2 Place filled crepe on baking sheet and place in oven to keep warm. Repeat with remaining crepes, cheese and ham.

3 To serve, place filled crepes on serving plates. Dollop with sour cream and garnish with chives or dill and, if desired, black pepper.

Stuff crepes with your favorite fillings.

tools
Measuring cups •
Baking sheet •
Medium skillet •
Serving plates •
Hot pads

DID YOU KNOW?

In France, Feb. 2 is known as *le jour des crêpes*, or the day of crepes. It's a French tradition to eat crepes on this day. Some hold a coin in one hand while flipping a crepe with the other. If they catch the crepe in the pan, they will have good luck!

HIDDEN HEALTHY

BEING A LITTLE SNEAKY ISN'T ALWAYS A BAD THING. THESE KID-FAVORITE FOODS GET A NUTRITIONAL BOOST FROM SECRET INGREDIENTS.

Cauliflower is a perfect substitute crust if you're gluten-free, too.

❤ Cauli Crust Pepperoni Pizza

MAKES 4 SERVINGS

WHAT YOU NEED

For the crust

- 4 cups cauliflower florets
- 1 egg, slightly beaten
- ¼ cup shredded part-skim mozzarella cheese
- ¼ cup grated Parmesan cheese
- ¼ cup plain panko breadcrumbs
- ¼ teaspoon dried oregano, crushed
- ¼ teaspoon dried basil leaves
- ¼ teaspoon salt

For the toppings

- ¾ cup no-sugar-added pizza sauce
- 1 cup shredded part-skim mozzarella cheese
- 3 ounces turkey pepperoni

HOW TO MAKE IT

1 Place a pizza stone or baking sheet in oven. Preheat oven to 425 F.

2 To make crust, in container of a food processor, add cauliflower; pulse until crumbly, with the texture of couscous. In casserole dish, place cauliflower and 2 tablespoons water. Cover and microwave 5 to 6 minutes or until cauliflower is tender, stirring once or twice. Let cool.

3 Transfer cauliflower to a clean, 100% cotton kitchen towel. Roll up towel. Hold towel over sink; twist and squeeze out as much water as you can (this step is very important so the crust gets crispy).

4 In a medium bowl, stir together cauliflower, egg, mozzarella, Parmesan, breadcrumbs, oregano, basil and salt. Transfer mixture to a piece of parchment paper. Pat and press into a 12-inch circle. Transfer crust (on parchment) to pizza stone. Bake 12 to 15 minutes or until crust is crisp and beginning to brown.

5 To top pizza, spread pizza sauce over crust. Sprinkle with cheese. Arrange turkey pepperoni on cheese. Bake 8 minutes or until cheese is melted and starting to bubble. Use a pizza cutter to slice pizza to serve.

tools

Pizza stone or baking sheet • Food processor • Measuring spoons • Measuring cups • Casserole dish • Kitchen towel • Medium bowl • Pizza cutter • Hot pads

⬇

tools

2 baking sheets • Sharp knife •
Resealable plastic bag •
Measuring spoons • Colander •
Paper towels • Hot pads •
2 large bowls • Spatula •
Blender or food
processor • Nonstick
skillet

Cheeseburgers With Crispy Sweet Potato Fries

MAKES 6 SERVINGS

WHAT YOU NEED

For the fries

Olive oil cooking spray
2 large sweet potatoes, peeled and cut into ¼ x ¼-inch sticks*
4 teaspoons cornstarch, divided
2 tablespoons canola or peanut oil, divided
Salt

For the burgers

½ cup canned chickpeas, drained and rinsed
2-3 teaspoons water
1 pound lean ground beef
½ cup rolled oats, ground in a food processor
2 tablespoons ketchup
1 teaspoon salt
Ground black pepper
6 thin slices cheddar cheese
6 whole-grain hamburger buns
Optional toppings: lettuce, tomato, ketchup, mustard, pickles

Chickpeas add extra fiber and key nutrients with each bite!

HOW TO MAKE IT

1 To make fries, preheat oven to 425 F. Line 2 large rimmed baking sheets with foil and spray with cooking spray.

2 In a large resealable plastic bag, place half of sweet potato sticks. Sprinkle with 2 teaspoons cornstarch. Seal bag, removing as much air as possible. Shake bag vigorously to coat fries. In a large bowl, pour fries; toss with 1 tablespoon oil. On 1 sheet, arrange fries in a single layer, leaving space between them. Repeat with remaining sweet potatoes, cornstarch and oil.

3 Bake 15 minutes, then use hot pads to remove trays from oven. Flip fries, keeping them in a single layer. Return pans to oven, rotating them and swapping shelves. Bake an additional 10 to 15 minutes or until browned and cooked through. Turn off oven and slightly open oven door to allow fries to crisp up an additional 10 minutes. Season with salt to taste.

4 Meanwhile, to make burgers, in a blender or food processor, combine chickpeas and 2 teaspoons water. Cover and process until very smooth, adding more water if necessary. (Not wet, just very smooth). In a large bowl, mix beef, pureed chickpeas, ground oats, ketchup, salt and pepper to taste. Gently mix until well combined. Shape into 6 thin patties.

5 Spray a nonstick skillet with cooking spray. Heat over medium-high heat. Cook burgers 3 to 4 minutes per side, then flip again and top with cheese. Cook an additional 2 to 3 minutes or until cheese is melted.

6 Serve burgers on buns with desired toppings and sweet potato fries.

* For best results, soak sweet potato sticks in cold water in the refrigerator at least 1 hour or overnight. Drain in a colander, rinse with fresh cool water and pat dry with paper towels.

Sweet Potato Sloppy Joes

MAKES 6 SERVINGS

WHAT YOU NEED

1	medium sweet potato
1-2	tablespoons fresh orange juice
1	pound 93% lean ground turkey
1	tablespoon olive oil
½	yellow onion, chopped
½	green bell pepper, chopped
¾	cup ketchup
2	teaspoons yellow mustard
1	tablespoon brown sugar
1	clove garlic, minced
½	teaspoon salt
¼	teaspoon ground black pepper
6	whole-grain hamburger buns, split and toasted
	Dill pickle slices (optional)

HOW TO MAKE IT

1 Use a vegetable brush to scrub sweet potato under cool running water. Use a fork to prick skin five or six times. Place sweet potato on a microwave-safe plate and microwave 8 to 10 minutes or until tender, turning sweet potato halfway during cooking. Remove from microwave with hot pads; let cool until it is easy enough to handle. Cut in half lengthwise and scoop flesh into a bowl. Add 1 tablespoon orange juice and mash with a potato masher, adding more orange juice as needed to achieve a very smooth, fairly loose puree; set aside.
2 In a large nonstick skillet over medium-high heat, cook turkey until it is cooked through, using a wooden spoon to break up meat. Transfer turkey to a bowl. Wipe skillet clean with paper towels.
3 Lower heat to medium. Add oil, onion and green pepper to skillet; cook 3 to 4 minutes, or until vegetables are lightly browned, stirring occasionally.
4 Add the turkey to skillet. Stir in sweet potato puree, ketchup, mustard, brown sugar, garlic, salt and black pepper. Cook 3 to 5 minutes or until liquid is reduced.
5 Serve on toasted buns. If desired, top with pickles.

⬇
tools
Vegetable brush • Medium bowls • Measuring spoons • Potato masher • Large skillet • Fork • Microwave-safe plate • Citrus squeezer • Measuring cups • Sharp knife • Cutting board • Wooden spoon • Paper towels • Hot pads

Sweet potatoes add fiber for healthy digestion.

Squash puree makes the color even brighter.

Both pumpkin and squash are loaded with beta-carotene for healthy eyes.

tools

Oven-safe baking dish • Large saucepan • Large bowl • Small saucepan • Wire whisk • Measuring cups • Measuring spoons • Colander • Can opener • Hot pads

Crispy-Topped Mac and Cheese

MAKES 4 SERVINGS

WHAT YOU NEED

   Olive oil cooking spray
8 ounces chickpea, lentil or multigrain high-protein elbow macaroni
1 tablespoon butter
1 tablespoon white whole-wheat flour
1 cup 2% milk
⅛ teaspoon salt
1 cup finely shredded mild cheddar cheese
¼ cup finely shredded Parmesan cheese, divided
¾ cup canned butternut squash or pumpkin puree
2 tablespoons whole-wheat panko breadcrumbs
1 teaspoon olive oil

HOW TO MAKE IT

1 Preheat oven to 350 F. Spray a 1½-quart baking dish with cooking spray. In a large pot, cook macaroni according to package directions; drain. Transfer macaroni to a large bowl and set aside.

2 Meanwhile, in a small saucepan over medium heat, melt butter. Sprinkle flour over butter and cook, whisking constantly, 1 minute. Whisk in milk and salt. Bring to a simmer; reduce heat. Cook, whisking constantly, 2 minutes. Remove from heat.

3 Whisk cheddar cheese and 2 tablespoons of Parmesan cheese into milk mixture. Whisk butternut squash puree into milk mixture to make cheese sauce. Stir cheese sauce into macaroni. Transfer macaroni mixture to baking dish.

4 In a small bowl, combine breadcrumbs, remaining Parmesan cheese and oil. Sprinkle crumb mixture over macaroni. Cover baking dish with lid (or with foil).

5 Bake 15 minutes. Remove lid (or foil) with hot pads and bake an additional 10 to 15 minutes or until mac and cheese is bubbling and crumbs are lightly browned and crisp.

6 Let stand 5 to 8 minutes before serving.

tools
Vegetable brush •
Medium bowl • Measuring
spoons • Potato masher •
Large skillet • Measuring
cups • Fork • Microwave-
safe plate • Wooden
spoon • Hot pads

Sweet potatoes make
tacos even more tasty!

Turkey Tacos
MAKES 5 SERVINGS

WHAT YOU NEED

1	medium sweet potato
1-2	tablespoons orange juice
1	pound 93% lean ground turkey
1	(1.25-ounce) package taco seasoning
1	cup mild salsa
10	whole-grain corn and lentil taco shells
1	cup shredded Mexican blend cheese
	Guacamole
	Shredded lettuce

HOW TO MAKE IT

1 Use a vegetable brush to scrub sweet potato under cool running water. Use a fork to prick skin five or six times. Place sweet potato on a microwave-safe plate and microwave 8 to 10 minutes or until tender, turning sweet potato halfway during cooking. Remove from microwave with hot pads; let cool until it is easy enough to handle. Cut in half lengthwise and scoop flesh into a bowl. Add 1 tablespoon orange juice and mash with a potato masher, adding more orange juice as needed to achieve a very smooth, fairly loose puree; set aside.
2 In a large nonstick skillet over medium-high heat, cook turkey until it is cooked through, using a wooden spoon to break up meat; drain (have a grown-up help with this step) and discard drippings. Stir in taco seasoning, salsa and cooked sweet potato puree. Bring to a simmer. Cook 5 to 6 minutes or until thickened.
3 Spoon turkey mixture into taco shells. Top with cheese, guacamole and lettuce.

Spaghetti and Confetti Meatballs

MAKES 4 SERVINGS

tools

Baking sheet   Measuring cups   Measuring spoons   Wooden spoon   Large bowl   Large saucepan   Grater   Colander   Hot pads   Serving dish

WHAT YOU NEED

- 1 pound 93% lean ground turkey
- 1 large egg, slightly beaten
- 1 teaspoon Worcestershire sauce
- ¼ cup grated Parmesan cheese, plus additional for serving
- ¼ cup whole-wheat panko breadcrumbs
- ½ cup finely grated zucchini
- ½ cup finely grated carrot
- 1 teaspoon onion powder
- ½ teaspoon garlic powder
- ¾ teaspoon dried Italian seasoning
- ¼ teaspoon salt
- ¼ teaspoon ground black pepper
- 8 ounces chickpea, lentil or multigrain high-protein spaghetti
  No-sugar-added jarred marinara sauce, warmed
  Grated Parmesan cheese (optional)

HOW TO MAKE IT

1 Preheat oven to 400 F. Line a large rimmed baking sheet with parchment paper (or with foil sprayed with olive oil cooking spray).

2 In a large bowl, gently mix turkey, egg, Worcestershire sauce, ¼ cup Parmesan cheese, breadcrumbs, zucchini, carrot, onion powder, garlic powder, Italian seasoning, salt and pepper until well combined.

3 Shape mixture into 1-inch meatballs; place on baking sheet. Bake 20 minutes or until cooked through.

4 Meanwhile, in a large pot, cook spaghetti according to package directions; drain.

5 In a large bowl, toss spaghetti with desired amount of warm marinara sauce. Transfer to serving dish; top with meatballs. Sprinkle with additional Parmesan cheese, if desired.

Sneak extra veggies into the meatball mix.

Get more protein out of your pasta.

tools

Muffin pan • Paper or foil liners • 2 large mixing bowls • Wire whisk • Sifter • Wooden spoon • Measuring spoons • Wire cooling rack • Electric mixer • Measuring cups • Can opener • Hot pads

Frosting gets a makeover with Greek yogurt.

Chocolate Cupcakes With Creamy Yogurt Frosting

MAKES 12 CUPCAKES

WHAT YOU NEED

For the cupcakes

- ¾ cup plain soy milk
- ¾ cup granulated sugar
- ¼ cup canned pumpkin puree
- ¼ cup vegetable oil
- 1 teaspoon white or cider vinegar
- 1½ teaspoons vanilla extract
- 1 cup white whole-wheat flour
- ⅓ cup unsweetened cocoa powder
- ¾ teaspoon baking soda
- ½ teaspoon baking powder
- ¼ teaspoon salt

For the frosting

- ½ cup plain whole-milk Greek yogurt
- ½ cup unsweetened cocoa powder
- 1 teaspoon vanilla extract
- ¼ teaspoon ground cinnamon
- 3-4 cups powdered sugar
  Colored or chocolate sprinkles (optional)

HOW TO MAKE IT

1 Preheat oven to 350 F.
Line 12 cups of a muffin pan with paper or foil liners.
2 To make cupcakes, in a large mixing bowl, whisk together soy milk, sugar, pumpkin puree, oil, vinegar and vanilla. Set aside. In another large bowl, whisk together flour, cocoa powder, baking soda, baking powder and salt.
3 Sift dry ingredients over wet ingredients, stopping several times to stir. Continue stirring to remove all large lumps.
4 Divide batter evenly among muffin cups until they are about two-thirds full. Bake 20 minutes or until a toothpick inserted near the centers comes out clean. Remove cupcakes from pan and cool on a wire cooling rack.
5 To make frosting, in a large bowl, using an electric mixer on low speed, mix yogurt, cocoa, vanilla and cinnamon. Beat in enough powdered sugar to make a thick, spreadable frosting.
6 Frost cooled cupcakes. If desired, decorate with rainbow or chocolate sprinkles.

TURN THIS...INTO THIS!

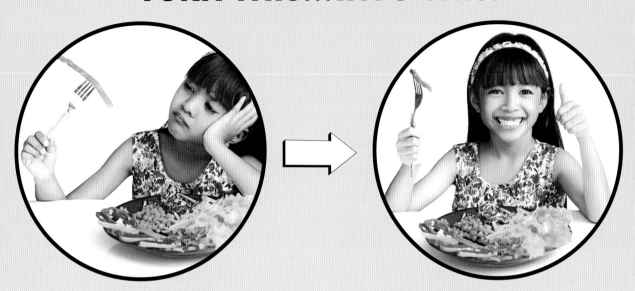

Hiding nutritious ingredients such as fruits and veggies, whole-grain products, legumes and yogurt in your kids' favorite foods is just one strategy to get them to eat healthy foods. The ultimate goal, of course, is to get them to truly crave those healthy foods. Here are a few tips to grow a good eater.

Start Early
When you first give your babies solid foods, start with pureed vegetables—and not necessarily the sweetest ones such as sweet potatoes, carrots and squash. Help them develop an appetite for vegetables of all kinds and not expect to exclusively eat sweet foods.

No Special Orders
When your children graduate to eating regular foods, make just one meal for the whole family. Don't make mac and cheese for the kids when the adults are eating grilled chicken and kale salad. Make healthy foods everyone will enjoy.

Eat as a Family
Life is busy, but research shows that if you can all sit down and eat together at least three or four nights a week, your children will have better nutrition habits and are less likely to get in trouble at school.

Don't Reward With Sweets
This can actually sabotage the healthy eating habits you're trying to teach your children. Giving sweets, chips or soda as a payoff can teach children to eat these foods to reward themselves when they're not hungry. Alternative rewards can include stickers, playing a favorite game or new art supplies.

Be a Cheerleader
Encourage them to try at least one bite of every food on their plate. No need to engage in an epic battle—but approach mealtime positively, with the expectation that your kids will at least try everything, and may just clean their plates.

Model Healthy Eating
If they see you eating and enjoying healthy foods, they'll want to eat them, too.

Cook Together
Even young children can do a little something to "help." Children are much more likely to eat something they've helped prepare.

Avoid Food Labels
Don't think "good" or "bad." Instead, connect healthy foods to things your children care about or to goals they may have—such as being strong for swimming, or doing well in school. Lean proteins help build muscles and brains. The vitamins, minerals and antioxidants in fruits and vegetables make your skin glow and your hair shiny.

Let Kids Have a Say
Have your kids taste the different foods on their plates and give them a grade— A, B, C, D or F. When they give high marks to healthy foods (especially vegetables!), serve them often.

$200

chapter 4

DELICIOUS DESSERTS

IT'S TIME FOR THE BEST PART OF THE MEAL!
EVERYONE WILL ENJOY THESE SPOON-LICKING TREATS.

75¢

FUN RAISER

BAKE SALES ARE A GREAT WAY TO RAISE MONEY FOR SCHOOL, SPORTS OR SOMETHING ELSE—BUT THESE TREATS ARE SO TASTY YOU'LL WANT TO KEEP AT LEAST A FEW FOR YOURSELF!

tools

Measuring cups • Measuring spoons • Three (5×3-inch) loaf pans • Pastry brush • Spoon • Large bowl • Silicone spatula • Toothpick • Hot pads • Small narrow metal spatula or table knife • Wire cooling rack • Can opener • Electric mixer

Pumpkin Spice Bread

Pumpkin Spice Bread

MAKES 3 LOAVES

WHAT YOU NEED

Shortening
1¾ cups all-purpose flour, plus extra for pans
1 cup canned pumpkin
¾ cup packed light brown sugar
½ cup butter, softened
2 eggs
2 teaspoons pumpkin pie spice
1 teaspoon baking soda
½ teaspoon salt
¼ teaspoon baking powder

HOW TO MAKE IT

1 Preheat oven to 350 F. Use a pastry brush to lightly spread shortening on bottoms and 1 inch up sides of 3 (5×3-inch) loaf pans. Sprinkle a spoonful of flour into each pan; shake pans to distribute flour evenly on greased bottoms and sides. Tap out and discard any excess flour. Place pans on a baking sheet; set aside.
2 In a large bowl, with an electric mixer on medium speed, beat 1¾ cups flour, pumpkin, brown sugar, butter, eggs, pumpkin pie spice, baking soda, salt and baking powder until well mixed. Turn off mixer; use a silicone spatula to scrape down sides of bowl.
3 Pour an equal amount of batter into each pan. Bake 35 to 45 minutes or until a toothpick inserted near centers comes out clean. Use hot pads to remove pans from oven.
4 Cool loaves 10 minutes in pans. Use a small narrow metal spatula or table knife to loosen sides of breads from pans. Remove from pans and cool completely on wire cooling racks before packaging for bake sale.

Individual Fruit Crisps

MAKES 6 TO 8 FRUIT CRISPS

WHAT YOU NEED

Nonstick cooking spray
2 (21-ounce) cans cherry, mixed berry, blueberry, strawberry, apple or peach pie filling
¾ cup packed brown sugar
½ cup all-purpose flour
½ cup old-fashioned rolled oats
⅓ cup butter or margarine, softened
¼ cup chopped pecans or almonds
1 teaspoon ground cinnamon
Whipped cream (optional)

HOW TO MAKE IT

1 Preheat oven to 375 F. Lightly spray 6 to 8 (3½- to 4-inch) foil tart pans with nonstick spray. Place pans on baking sheets.
2 Spoon pie filling into each pan.
3 In a small bowl, use a fork to mix brown sugar, flour, oats and cinnamon. Use a fork to mix in butter. Stir in nuts. Sprinkle over pie filling.
4 Bake 25 to 30 minutes or until topping is golden brown. Use hot pads to remove baking sheets from oven. Place fruit crisps on wire cooling racks to cool completely before packaging for bake sale. Top with whipped cream, if desired.

tools
Measuring cups • Measuring spoons • Can opener • 6 to 8 (3½- to 4-inch) foil tart pans • Baking sheets • Spoon • Small bowl • Fork • Hot pads • Wire cooling racks

No Bake Crispy Pops

MAKES 16 POPS

WHAT YOU NEED

For the cereal pops

1-2	tablespoons butter, softened
3	tablespoons butter
4	cups mini marshmallows
6	cups crispy rice cereal
16	wooden or paper cake-pop sticks

For the coating and decorations

1	cup white chocolate chips
2	teaspoons canola oil, divided
1	cup milk chocolate chips
	Sprinkles (optional)

HOW TO MAKE IT

1 To make cereal pops, place a large piece of foil in a 13×9-inch baking pan, extending foil over long edges of pan. Use a pastry brush to spread 1 to 2 tablespoons softened butter on bottom and sides of foil-lined pan. Set aside.

2 In a large saucepan over low heat, melt 3 tablespoons butter. Add mini marshmallows. Continue heating and stirring with a wooden spoon until marshmallows are melted.

3 Remove saucepan from heat. Add cereal. Stir until the cereal is completely coated.

4 Spoon cereal mixture into pan. Use silicone spatula to flatten cereal mixture into pan. Let cool completely.

5 Use foil to lift cereal mixture out of pan and place it on a cutting board. Remove foil. Cut cereal mixture into 16 equal rectangular pieces. Push a pop stick into each. (If desired, use fingers to push top corners down to round them like ice cream pops.)

6 Place a large piece of waxed paper or parchment paper on a baking sheet; set aside.

7 To make coating, in a microwave-safe bowl, place white chocolate chips and 1 teaspoon oil. Microwave 30 seconds; stir with a spoon. Microwave and stir in 30-second intervals until completely melted. Repeat in another bowl with milk chocolate chips and remaining oil.

8 Hold a cereal pop by the stick; dip it in melted white chocolate. Let excess drip off. Then either dip pop into milk chocolate, or use a spoon to drizzle it on. If you like, decorate with sprinkles before chocolate is dry. Repeat with remaining pops.

9 Place pops on prepared baking sheet. Refrigerate until chocolate is set before packaging for bake sale.

Caramel Pecan Popcorn

MAKES 4 CUPS

WHAT YOU NEED

	Nonstick cooking spray
1	(3.3-ounce) bag microwave popcorn
1	cup pecan halves
½	cup unsalted butter
1	cup packed light brown sugar
¼	cup light corn syrup
½	teaspoon salt
½	teaspoon baking soda

HOW TO MAKE IT

1 Preheat oven to 300 F. Lightly spray a 13×9-inch baking pan with nonstick spray.

2 In a microwave, pop popcorn according to package directions. Carefully open bag and pour popcorn into baking pan. Remove all unpopped kernels. Add pecans to pan; set aside.

3 To make caramel, in a medium saucepan over medium-high heat, melt butter. Use a wooden spoon to stir in brown sugar, corn syrup and salt. Bring mixture to boil. Boil 2 minutes, stirring constantly.

4 Remove saucepan from heat. Stir in baking soda (mixture will foam up). Pour caramel mixture over popcorn mixture. Stir with a wooden spoon until popcorn is evenly coated.

5 Bake 15 minutes, stirring every 5 minutes. Use hot pads to remove pan from oven; stir again. On a clean work surface, place a large piece of parchment paper. Spread caramel popcorn onto parchment and let cool completely before packaging for bake sale.

⬇
tools

Measuring cups • Measuring spoons • 13x9-inch baking pan • Foil • Pastry brush • Large saucepan • Wooden spoon • Silicone spatula • Cutting board • Sharp knife • Waxed paper • Wooden pop sticks • 2 Medium microwave-safe bowls • Hot pads

50¢

Simple DIY paper cones hold the treats.

⬇
tools
Measuring cups •
Measuring spoons •
Parchment paper •
13×9-inch baking pan •
Medium saucepan •
Wooden spoon •
Hot pads

⇩

tools

Measuring cups • Measuring spoons • Sharp knife • Cutting board • Egg separator • Muffin pan • Paper bake-cup liners • 2-cup measuring cup • 2 large bowls • Ice cream scoop or large spoon • Toothpick • Hot pads • Wire cooling racks • Small narrow spatula or table knife

Sprinkle with colored sugar to make these sparkle.

Strawberry Cupcakes With Strawberry Buttercream Frosting

MAKES 12 CUPCAKES

WHAT YOU NEED

For the cupcakes

12 ounces strawberries, cut up
¼ cup water
1 (15.25-ounce) package strawberry cake mix
3 egg whites
⅓ cup vegetable oil

For the frosting

1 stick butter (½ cup), softened
2 tablespoons seedless strawberry jam
½ teaspoon almond flavoring
2 cups powdered sugar
1 to 2 tablespoons milk (optional)
  Red food coloring
  Pink or red decorating sugar (optional)

HOW TO MAKE IT

1 Preheat oven to 350 F. Line 12 (2½-inch) cups of a muffin pan with paper cup liners. Set aside.

2 In a blender, place strawberries and water. Cover and blend by turning blender on and off several times until mixture is smooth. Pour strawberry mixture into a 2-cup measuring cup. You should have 1¾ cups. If not, add enough water to equal 1¾ cups.

3 In a large bowl, with an electric mixer on medium speed, beat cake mix, strawberry mixture, egg whites and oil 2 to 3 minutes or until well mixed. Use an ice cream scoop or spoon to scoop batter into muffin cups, filling each about three-fourths full.

4 Bake 18 to 25 minutes or until a toothpick inserted near center comes out clean. Use hot pads to remove pan from oven. Remove cupcakes from muffin cups; let cool completely on wire cooling racks.

5 To make frosting, in a large clean bowl, with an electric mixer on medium speed, beat butter 2 minutes. Beat in strawberry jam and almond flavoring.

6 Turn mixer to low speed. Slowly add powdered sugar; beat 3 to 5 minutes or until creamy. If frosting is too stiff for spreading, beat in 1 to 2 tablespoons milk. Beat in a drop or more of red food coloring to tint the frosting pink.

7 Use a small narrow spatula or table knife to spread frosting on cool cupcakes. If you like, sprinkle with decorating sugar.

Butterscotch Snickerdoodles

MAKES 42 COOKIES

WHAT YOU NEED

1 (15.25-ounce) package white cake mix
1 stick (½ cup) butter, melted
1 egg
1 cup butterscotch chips
3 tablespoons white sugar
1½ teaspoons ground cinnamon

HOW TO MAKE IT

1 Preheat oven to 350 F.

2 In a large bowl, use a wooden spoon to stir cake mix, butter and egg until dough forms. Stir in butterscotch chips.

3 In a small bowl, use a spoon to stir together sugar and cinnamon.

4 Roll dough into 1-inch balls. Roll each ball in cinnamon-sugar mixture. Place balls about 2 inches apart on ungreased baking sheets.

5 Bake 10 to 12 minutes or until set. Use hot pads to remove sheets from oven. Use a pancake turner to remove cookies from sheet and place on wire cooling racks. Cool completely before packaging for bake sale.

tools

Measuring cups • Measuring spoons • Large bowl • Wooden spoon • Small bowl • Small spoon • Baking sheets • Hot pads • Pancake turner • Wire cooling racks

Chocolate Chip Switcheroo Make Butterscotch Snickerdoodles as directed above, except use 1 cup chocolate chips instead of the butterscotch chips, and do not roll the balls in cinnamon-sugar mixture.

MAKE-IT-YOURSELF
BIRTHDAY CAKES

CELEBRATE THE SPECIAL DAY WITH A FUN AND FESTIVE DESSERT
THAT'S SURE TO PLEASE EVERYONE AT THE PARTY!

"I MADE IT MYSELF!"

HAPPY BIRTHDAY TO ME!

Chocolate Party Cake

WHAT YOU NEED

- 3 cups all-purpose flour, divided
- 2 cups white sugar, divided
- ½ cup unsweetened cocoa powder, divided
- 2 teaspoons baking soda
- ½ teaspoon salt
- ¾ cup canola oil
- 2 tablespoons cider vinegar
- 1 tablespoon vanilla extract
- 2 cups cold water
  Favorite ready-to-spread frosting
  Cake decorations

HOW TO MAKE IT

1 Preheat oven to 350 F. Place a large wire strainer in a 13×9-inch baking pan or dish (select a nice pan, because you will be serving the cake in the pan!). Put 1 cup flour, 1 cup sugar, ¼ cup cocoa, baking soda and salt in strainer. Hold strainer slightly above pan. Use a spoon to stir ingredients so they are sifted into pan. Repeat sifting with remaining flour, sugar and cocoa. Stir mixture until well combined.

2 Use a spoon to make three holes in flour mixture. In the first hole, pour oil. In the second hole, pour vinegar. In the third hole, pour vanilla. Pour water over mixture. Stir with a fork or wire whisk until well combined.

3 Bake 35 to 40 minutes or until a toothpick inserted near center of cake comes out clean. Use hot pads to remove cake from oven. Place pan on wire cooling rack; let cake cool completely.

4 Use a small spatula or table knife to spread frosting on top of cake. Decorate as desired.

tools

13x9-inch baking pan or dish • Measuring cups • Measuring spoons • Large wire strainer • Spoon • Hot pads • Wire cooling rack • Small narrow spatula or table knife

Cookie-Cutter Stenciling

What you need

- ☐ Ready-to-spread frosting
- ☐ Alphabet cookie cutters
- ☐ Assorted colored sprinkles and/or decorating sugars

How to do it

- ☐ Let cake cool completely.
- ☐ Use a small spatula to spread frosting on top of cake.
- ☐ Freeze cake for 30 minutes to slightly firm up the frosting.
- ☐ Gently press cookie cutters into frosting. Gently sprinkle colored sprinkles or sugars inside each cutter.
- ☐ Carefully lift cutters straight off the frosting.

Start with this basic 13x9-inch cake, then decorate it with one of the fun designs on the following pages—or one you create yourself!

Cake and candy!

Birthday Party at the Beach Cake

WHAT YOU NEED

- Ready-to-spread white frosting
- Blue liquid food coloring
- Graham cracker crumbs
- Laffy Taffy candies and/or fruit leather
- Gummy Life Savers and Trolli Peachie O's candies
- Mini Swedish Fish and/or gummy fish
- Teddy Grahams
- Goldfish crackers
- Cocktail umbrellas
- Pebble rocks candies (optional)
- Decorating frosting, gels or letters for making a message on cake (optional)

HOW TO MAKE IT

1 Make the Chocolate Party Cake on p. 105. Let cake cool completely.

2 Put frosting in a bowl. Stir in a few drops of blue food coloring.

3 Use a small spatula or table knife to spread frosting on top of cake, making swirls to look like waves.

4 Sprinkle graham cracker crumbs on one half of the cake for sand. Shape taffy or cut fruit leather to make beach blankets and a volleyball net. Let the photo inspire your creativity as you decorate the cake with cocktail umbrellas, candies and crackers.

Rainbow Birthday Party Cake

WHAT YOU NEED
- Ready-to-spread white frosting
- M&M's, Skittles or other small round colored candies
- Cotton candy
- Blue decorating sugar
- Decorating frosting, gels or letters for making a message on cake (optional)

HOW TO MAKE IT
1 Make the Chocolate Party Cake on p. 105. Let cake cool completely.
2 Use a small spatula or table knife to spread frosting on top of cake.
3 Gently press candies into frosting to form a rainbow.
4 Place mounds of cotton candy "clouds" on the bottom of each side of the rainbow. Sprinkle "sky" with blue sugar.

Easy designs make it fun.

Peach and Berry Yogurt Parfait

MAKES 1 SERVING

tools
Measuring cups •
Measuring spoons •
Parfait glass

WHAT YOU NEED
- 1 cup vanilla Greek yogurt
- ½ cup frozen peaches, thawed
- ¼ cup granola
- ¼ cup fresh raspberries
- ¼ cup fresh blueberries
- 1 tablespoon sliced almonds (optional)
- Honey

HOW TO MAKE IT
1 In a parfait glass, layer yogurt, peaches and granola.
2 Top with raspberries, blueberries and, if you like, almonds. Drizzle with honey.

I SCREAM! YOU SCREAM!
FOR FRUIT & YOGURT!

ENJOY THESE TASTY TWISTS ON
YOUR FAVORITE ICE CREAM PARLOR TREATS.
BEST OF ALL, THEY'RE HEALTHFUL, TOO.

Yogurt Banana Split

MAKES 1 SERVING

WHAT YOU NEED

½ cup reduced-fat vanilla or strawberry-banana yogurt

1 medium banana

¼ cup blackberries or blueberries

¼ cup raspberries or chopped strawberries

½ cup granola

1 tablespoon honey

1 maraschino cherry

HOW TO MAKE IT

1 Place container of yogurt in freezer 30 minutes, or until slightly firm.

2 Unpeel banana. Cut in half lengthwise. In a banana-split dish or breakfast bowl, place banana halves.

3 Use a small ice cream scoop or spoon to scoop yogurt onto banana halves.

4 Top with berries and granola. Drizzle with honey and put a cherry on top.

tools

Measuring spoons • Measuring cups • Sharp knife • Cutting board • Banana-split dish or breakfast bowl • Small ice cream scoop or spoon

Berry delicious!

Fruit 'n' Yogurt Sundae Bowls

MAKES 4 SERVINGS

WHAT YOU NEED

- 4 waffle bowls
- ⅓ cup chopped kiwi
- ⅓ cup chopped fresh strawberries
- ⅓ cup fresh blueberries
- ¼ cup toasted oats cereal, divided
- 2 cups favorite-flavor Greek yogurt
- 1 tablespoon sweetened flaked coconut
- 1 tablespoon toasted sliced almonds
- 1 tablespoon colored sprinkles, mini chocolate chips, dried cranberries and/or dried mixed fruit bits
- 4 strawberry halves

HOW TO MAKE IT

1 In waffle bowls, add equal amounts of kiwi, strawberries and blueberries.
2 Sprinkle a teaspoon of cereal on each bowl; top each with an equal amount of yogurt.
3 Sprinkle each bowl with equal amounts of remaining cereal, coconut, almonds and sprinkles or other toppings. Garnish each bowl with a strawberry half and serve.

tools

Measuring cups •
Measuring spoons •
Sharp knife •
Cutting board •
Spoon

Two treats in one—a fruit sundae plus a crispy cookie bowl.

A fun treat for breakfast, too!

tools
Measuring cups • Measuring spoons • Frozen-pop molds • 3 medium resealable plastic bags • Rolling pin • Medium bowl • Spoon • Scissors • Small bowl • Food processor

Cherry Chocolate Yogurt Pops

MAKES ABOUT 6 POPS

WHAT YOU NEED

- 7-8 chocolate graham cracker squares
- 16 ounces frozen dark sweet pitted cherries, slightly thawed
- 1 tablespoon white sugar
- 2 cups reduced-fat vanilla yogurt
- ¼ cup whole milk
  Frozen-pop molds
- 6 wooden ice pop sticks

HOW TO MAKE IT

1 In a medium resealable plastic bag, place graham crackers. Seal bag. Use rolling pin to crush crackers into fine crumbs. (You should have ½ cup crumbs.) Pour into small bowl; set aside.

2 In the container of a food processor, add cherries; sprinkle with sugar. Cover and process until smooth. Stir 1 tablespoon cherry mixture into chocolate crumbs until slightly moistened. Pour remaining cherry mixture into a medium resealable bag. Seal bag.

3 In a medium bowl, use a spoon to stir together yogurt and milk. Spoon yogurt mixture into a resealable bag. Seal bag.

4 Use scissors to snip off a lower corner from yogurt and cherry bags.

5 Fill pop molds, starting with yogurt, then cherry mixture, then crumbs. Insert sticks and freeze at least 6 hours or until firm.

6 To serve, remove pops from freezer and let stand 5 minutes. Remove pops from molds.

chapter 5

A YEAR OF YUM!

FIND TREATS SWEET OR SAVORY THAT YOU
CAN MAKE TOGETHER EVERY MONTH.

Candy corn
and cupcakes—
a perfect
Halloween treat!

HOLIDAY PARTY FUN

CELEBRATE FESTIVE OCCASIONS WITH A CALENDAR'S WORTH OF GOODIES.

New Year's Day

January
Confetti Snack Mix
MAKES ABOUT 4½ CUPS

WHAT YOU NEED

- 4½ cups toasted rice squares cereal
- 1 (10- or 11-ounce) package white chocolate chips
- ¼ cup butter
- 3 tablespoons heavy whipping cream
- 1 teaspoon vanilla extract
- ⅔ cup rainbow sprinkles
- 1½ cups powdered sugar

HOW TO MAKE IT

1 In a large bowl, place cereal.

2 In a medium saucepan over low heat, melt white chocolate chips, butter and cream, stirring occasionally. (The mixture will be very thick and buttery.) Remove from heat. Stir in vanilla.

3 While still warm, pour white chocolate mixture over cereal. Gently stir with a wooden spoon until cereal is coated. Immediately scatter sprinkles over cereal. Gently toss with wooden spoon just until mixed. (Do not overmix or the sprinkles will lose their color.)

4 In a large resealable plastic bag, place powdered sugar. Pour cereal into bag. Seal bag. Shake until cereal is coated with sugar.

5 Throw away powdered sugar that did not stick to the cereal. Store at room temperature for up to 2 weeks.

⬇ tools
Measuring cups • Measuring spoons • Large bowl • Medium saucepan • Wooden spoon • Large resealable plastic bag

February
Red Velvet Ice Cream Sandwiches

MAKES 20 ICE CREAM SANDWICHES

WHAT YOU NEED

- 1 (15.25-ounce) package red velvet cake mix
- ⅓ cup vegetable oil
- 2 eggs
- ½ cup sprinkles
- 4 cups vanilla ice cream

HOW TO MAKE IT

1 Preheat oven to 350 F. Line 2 baking sheets with parchment. Set aside.

2 In a large bowl, use a wooden spoon to stir together cake mix, oil and eggs until dough forms (dough will be stiff).

3 Roll dough into 1-inch balls. Place about 2 inches apart on baking sheets.

4 Bake cookies 8 to 10 minutes or until set around the edges. Use hot pads to remove sheets from oven. Let cookies cool 1 minute on baking sheets. Use a pancake turner to place cookies on wire cooling racks. Let cookies cool completely.

5 To assemble ice cream sandwiches, put sprinkles into a shallow dish. Working quickly, place a small scoop (about 3 to 4 tablespoons) of ice cream on the bottom sides of half of the cookies. Top with remaining cookies, bottom sides down. Press together lightly; roll edges of ice cream sandwiches in sprinkles.

6 Immediately place ice cream sandwiches on a tray. Freeze 2 to 3 hours or until firm.

7 When ice cream is firm, put ice cream sandwiches into a tightly covered container, or wrap each sandwich in plastic wrap. Store in freezer up to 1 month.

⬇
tools

Measuring cups • Measuring spoons • Parchment paper • 2 baking sheets • Large bowl • Wooden spoon • Hot pads • Pancake turner • Wire cooling racks • Ice cream scoop • Shallow dish • Tray • Rolling pin

Valentine's Day

Saint Patrick's Day

tools

Measuring cups • Large
bowl • Wooden spoon •
Small saucepan •
13x9-inch baking pan •
2-inch shamrock-shaped
cookie cutter •
Plastic wrap

March

Shamrock Jewels

MAKES 10 TO 12

WHAT YOU NEED

- 3 (3-ounce) boxes lime-flavored gelatin
- 4 (7-gram) envelopes unflavored gelatin
- 2 cups boiling water
- 2 cups white grape or apple juice
  Color decorating sugars (optional)

HOW TO MAKE IT

1 In a large bowl, use a wooden spoon to stir together lime-flavor and unflavored gelatins.

2 Pour boiling water over gelatin. Use a wooden spoon to stir at least 3 minutes to completely dissolve gelatin. Stir in juice.

3 Pour gelatin mixture into a 13×9-inch baking pan. Refrigerate at least 3 hours or until firm.

4 Dip bottom of pan in warm water for 15 seconds. Use a 2-inch shamrock-shaped cookie cutter to cut gelatin into shamrocks. Be sure to cut all the way through the gelatin to the bottom of the pan.

5 Carefully lift the shamrocks from the pan and place them on a platter (or arrange them onto small pieces of parchment paper, for easy serving). Save the gelatin scraps for snacking.

6 Cover shamrocks with plastic wrap and refrigerate until serving or up to 4 hours. If you like, just before serving, sprinkle with colored sugars.

April
Swirly Hot Dog Snakes

MAKES 12 HOT DOG SNAKES

WHAT YOU NEED

　　Nonstick cooking spray
2　(11-ounce containers) refrigerated breadstick dough
12　hot dogs
12　tiny strips sliced pimientos
1　egg, beaten
2　tablespoons grated Parmesan cheese
24　dried currants
　　Finely chopped fresh basil

HOW TO MAKE IT

1 Preheat oven to 375 F. Lightly spray two baking sheets with nonstick spray. Set aside.

2 Open breadstick containers and remove dough, but do not unroll. Separate dough from each container into 6 coils at perforations (12 coils total).

3 To make each snake, unroll 1 coil. Press center perforation to seal, making one 12-inch-long breadstick. Repeat for each coil.

4 Wrap a breadstick around each hot dog in a spiral fashion, leaving about 2 inches overhanging at each end. Place on prepared baking sheets.

5 Use kitchen scissors to snip one end of dough to make a mouth slit. Insert 1 pimiento slice into each mouth for a tongue. Use a fork to press other end of dough to resemble a rattle.

6 Use a pastry brush to brush beaten egg on each snake. Sprinkle with cheese. To make eyes, press 2 currants into dough above tongue.

7 Bake 14 to 17 minutes or until golden brown. Use a pancake turner to remove snakes from baking sheet; place on tray. Sprinkle with basil.

tools
Measuring spoons •
Small bowl • Fork • Sharp
knife • Cutting board •
2 baking sheets • Kitchen
scissors • Pastry brush •
Pancake turner •
Hot pads

April Fool's Day

May
Flowerpot Cupcakes
MAKES 24 CUPCAKES

Mother's Day

WHAT YOU NEED
For the cupcakes
- 1 16.5-ounce package yellow cake mix
  Fresh orange juice (enough to replace water in cake mix)
- 2 teaspoons grated orange peel
- ½ teaspoon vanilla extract

For the frosting
- 1 16-ounce container ready-to-spread vanilla frosting
- 1 tablespoon powdered sugar
- 1 tablespoon fresh orange juice
- ½ teaspoon grated orange peel

For the marshmallow flowers
- Nonstick cooking spray
- 30 large marshmallows
- 24 small gumdrops or candy-coated almonds
- Decorating sugars in assorted colors

tools
Measuring cups • Measuring spoons • Citrus squeezer • Citrus zester • 2 muffin pans • Paper bake-cup liners • Large bowl • Ice cream scoop or large spoon • Toothpick • Hot pads • Wire cooling racks • Medium bowl • Wooden spoon • Small narrow spatula or table knife • Kitchen scissors

HOW TO MAKE IT
1 Preheat oven to 350 F. Line 24 (2½-inch) cups of 2 muffin pans with cup liners. Set aside.
2 To make cupcakes, make batter according to package directions, replacing water with orange juice and adding orange peel and vanilla. Use ice cream scoop or spoon to fill each cup three-quarters full with batter.
3 Bake 18 to 25 minutes or until a toothpick inserted in center comes out clean. Use hot pads to remove pans from oven. Remove cupcakes from muffin cups; cool completely on wire cooling racks.
4 To make frosting, in a medium bowl, add ready-to-spread frosting. Use a wooden spoon to stir in remaining frosting ingredients; stir until thoroughly mixed. Use a small narrow spatula or table knife to spread frosting on cupcakes.
5 To make marshmallow flowers, spray blades of kitchen scissors with nonstick spray. Cut each marshmallow crosswise into four slices. Sprinkle one side of cut surface with colored sugar. (Or press one side of cut marshmallows in dish of colored sugar.) Arrange 5 slices on each cupcake in a flower shape. Place gumdrop or almond in center of each flower. Loosely cover until serving.

⬇
tools

Measuring cups ● Measuring
spoons ● 6-cup popover pan
or 6 (6-ounce) custard cups ●
Baking sheet ● Small bowl ●
Spoon ● Medium bowl ●
Wire whisk ● Hot pads ●
Wire cooling rack ●
Pastry brush

June
Popovers for Pop

MAKES 6 POPOVERS

WHAT YOU NEED

Nonstick cooking spray
¼ cup white sugar
1 teaspoon ground cinnamon
¼ teaspoon ground cloves
¼ teaspoon ground nutmeg
2 eggs
1 cup all-purpose flour
1 cup milk
½ teaspoon salt
½ stick (¼ cup) butter, melted

HOW TO MAKE IT

1 Preheat oven to 450 F. Generously spray a 6-cup
popover pan or 6 (6-ounce) custard cups with nonstick
spray. If using custard cups, place cups on a baking
sheet. Set popover pan or custard cups aside.

2 In a small bowl, use spoon to stir sugar, cinnamon,
cloves and nutmeg until mixed. Set aside.

3 In a medium bowl, crack eggs. Use a wire whisk to
beat eggs well. Add flour, milk and salt. Whisk just
until smooth (do not overwhisk). Stir in 1 tablespoon
of sugar-cinnamon mixture.

4 Fill cups about half full with batter. Bake
20 minutes. Reduce oven temperature to 350 F.
Bake 20 minutes more or until golden brown.

5 Use hot pads to remove pan from oven.
Immediately remove popovers from cups. Place
popovers on a wire cooling rack. Use a pastry
brush to lightly brush popovers with melted
butter. Sprinkle with remaining sugar-cinnamon
mixture. Serve hot.

Father's Day

⬇
tools
Measuring cups • Serrated knife • Cutting board • Table knife • 1¼-inch star-shaped cookie cutter • 4 (8-ounce) parfait glasses • Spoons

July

Stars and Stripes Berry-Coconut Parfaits
MAKES 4 SERVINGS

WHAT YOU NEED
- 1 (10¾-ounce) loaf frozen pound cake
- ¼ cup raspberry jelly
- 2 cups fresh blueberries
- 2 (6-ounce) containers low-fat coconut yogurt
- ½ cup shredded coconut, toasted

HOW TO MAKE IT
1 Use a serrated knife to cut 14 (¼-inch) slices of pound cake. (Return remaining cake to freezer and save for another use.)
2 Use a table knife to spread 7 slices with jelly. Top each jelly slice with a plain slice to make cake sandwiches. Use serrated knife to trim crusts from sandwiches. (If you like, save scrapes for snacking.)
3 Using a 1¼-inch star-shaped cookie cutter, cut 4 sandwiches into stars. Set stars aside.
4 Cut remaining sandwiches into ¾-inch squares.
5 To assemble parfaits, in four 8-ounce parfait glasses, layer half each of cake squares, blueberries and yogurt. Repeat layers. Sprinkle with coconut. Top each parfait with a cake star to serve.

tools

Measuring cups • Measuring spoons • 9-inch square baking pan • Medium bowl • Wooden spoon • Large bowl • Electric mixer • Small metal spoon • Hot pads • Wire cooling rack • Sharp knife

August

S'mores Blondies

MAKES 12 TO 15 BARS

WHAT YOU NEED

Nonstick cooking spray
1⅓ cups all-purpose flour
¾ cup graham cracker crumbs
1 teaspoon baking powder
1 stick (½ cup) butter, softened
¾ cup packed brown sugar
1 egg
1 teaspoon vanilla extract
2 cups milk chocolate chips
1 (7-ounce jar) marshmallow creme
1½ graham crackers

HOW TO MAKE IT

1 Preheat oven to 350 F. Lightly spray a 9-inch square baking pan with nonstick spray. Set aside.
2 In a medium bowl, use wooden spoon to stir flour, graham cracker crumbs and baking powder together until mixed. Set flour mixture aside.

3 In a large bowl, use an electric mixer on medium to cream butter and brown sugar until fluffy. Add egg and vanilla. Beat again until well mixed.
4 Set aside ½ cup flour mixture for topping. Add remaining flour mixture to butter mixture. Beat on low speed until mixed into a dough.
5 Press dough into baking pan. Sprinkle chocolate chips on top.
6 Spoon small amounts of marshmallow creme on top of chocolate chips. Use back of spoon to spread creme to cover chocolate chips. Sprinkle with reserved flour mixture.
7 Break the 1½ graham crackers into small pieces. Sprinkle on top of marshmallow layer.
8 Bake 25 to 30 minutes, or until golden brown. Use hot pads to remove pan from oven. Let cool completely on a wire cooling rack. Cut into bars.

September
Pizza Faces

MAKES 4 PIZZAS

WHAT YOU NEED

- 2 round sandwich thins or pita bread rounds, split
- ½ cup pizza sauce
- ½ cup shredded Italian cheese blend
  Toppings: mini pepperoni slices; sliced fresh mushrooms, black olives, tomatoes, bell peppers and/or other vegetables

HOW TO MAKE IT

1 Preheat oven to 375 F. Place each half of a sandwich thin or pita round on a separate serving plate for "crusts."

2 For each pizza face, have each guest use a small spoon to spread 1 to 2 tablespoons pizza sauce on their crust. Sprinkle with 2 tablespoons cheese. Use assorted vegetables to create faces.

3 Place pizza paces on a baking sheet. Bake 5 to 8 minutes or until cheese melts. Use hot pads to remove baking sheet from oven. Use a pancake turner to place each pizza face on a guest's plate.

⬇
tools

Measuring cups • Measuring spoons • Sharp knife • Cutting board • 4 serving plates • 4 small spoons • Small bowls for toppings • Baking sheet • Hot pads • Pancake turner

Back-to-School Pizza Party

Halloween

October
Halloween Sausage Mummies

MAKES 12 MUMMIES

WHAT YOU NEED
- ½ (17.3-ounce) package frozen puff pastry sheets (1 sheet), thawed
- 12 bun-length fully cooked sausages or hot dogs
- 1 egg, slightly beaten
  Small squeeze bottles of ketchup and yellow mustard, or tiny cheese cutouts and chopped black olives

HOW TO MAKE IT
1 Preheat oven to 425 F. Line a baking sheet with parchment paper. Set aside.

2 Use a pizza cutter to cut pastry sheets into ¼- to ½-inch-wide strips. Wrap strips randomly around each sausage to resemble bandages. Leave a gap at one end for creating the face later. Place wrapped sausages on baking sheet, leaving space around each "mummy."

3 Use a pastry brush to lightly brush pastry with beaten egg. Bake 12 to 15 minutes or until pastry is puffed and golden.

4 Use hot pads to remove baking sheet from oven. Use a pancake turner to remove mummies from the baking sheet and place on a tray to decorate.

5 Make eyes on mummies with small dots of mustard or cheese cutouts, topped with dots of ketchup or olive pieces for pupils; then serve.

Happy Thanksgiving!

tools

Measuring cups • Measuring spoons • Can opener • (3) 2½-inch muffin pans (36 cups) • Paper cupcake liners • Large bowl • Wire whisk • Medium bowl • Wooden spoon • Ice cream scoop or large spoon • Toothpick • Hot pads • Wire cooling racks

November
Pumpkin Butterscotch Muffins

MAKES 36 MUFFINS

WHAT YOU NEED

Nonstick cooking spray
1½ cups all-purpose flour
1½ cups whole-wheat flour
2 teaspoons baking soda
2 teaspoons baking powder
1 teaspoon pumpkin pie spice
½ teaspoon salt
4 eggs, slightly beaten
2 cups white sugar
1 (15-ounce) can pumpkin puree
1 cup vegetable oil
1 teaspoon vanilla extract
2 cups butterscotch chips

HOW TO MAKE IT

1 Preheat oven to 350 F. Line 36 (2½-inch) cups of muffin pans with cup liners. Set aside.

2 In a large bowl, use a wire whisk to stir together all-purpose flour, whole-wheat flour, baking soda, baking powder, pumpkin pie spice and salt until mixed. Make a hole in center of flour mixture. Set aside.

3 In a medium bowl, use a wire whisk to beat eggs. Add sugar, pumpkin puree, oil and vanilla. Stir with wire whisk to mix well. Pour pumpkin mixture into center of flour mixture. Stir with a wooden spoon just until mixed (batter will be lumpy). Gently stir in butterscotch chips.

4 Use an ice cream scoop or spoon to scoop batter into muffin cups.

5 Bake 20 to 25 minutes or until a toothpick inserted near the centers of the muffins comes out clean. Use hot pads to remove pan from oven. Cool muffins in muffin cups 5 minutes. Remove muffins from cups; serve warm or at room temperature.

December
Snowflake Cookies

MAKES 12 TO 14 COOKIES

WHAT YOU NEED

- **1** (16.5-ounce) roll refrigerated sugar cookie dough
- **½** cup (8 tablespoons) flour, plus additional flour for rolling out

For the frosting

- **1** (14-ounce) container ready-to-spread royal icing or white frosting
  Ready-to-use cookie icing
  White decorating or coarse-grain sugar (optional)

HOW TO MAKE IT

1 To make cookies, on a clean cutting board, break cookie dough roll into small pieces. Sprinkle with 3 to 4 tablespoons flour and use clean hands to work flour into dough. Continue adding flour 3 to 4 tablespoons at a time until all the flour is mixed in. If dough is too soft to roll out, cover and refrigerate 10 to 15 minutes.

2 Lightly sprinkle cutting board with flour. Roll dough to ¼-inch thickness. Use 1½- to 2 ½-inch snowflake- or flower-shaped cookie cutters. Use pancake turner to carefully remove cookies from cutting board and place 2 inches apart on ungreased baking sheet.

3 Freeze cookies on the baking sheet at least 30 minutes (This will help them maintain their shape.)

4 Preheat oven to 350 F. Bake 8 to 12 minutes or until edges are very lightly browned. Use a pancake turner to remove cookies from baking sheet; place on a wire cooling rack to cool completely.

5 Decorate cookies with icing, frosting and/or sugar.

Winter Wonderland Party

tools

Measuring cups   Measuring spoons   Cutting board   Baking sheet   Rolling pin   1½- to 2½-inch snowflake- or flower-shaped cookie cutters   Pancake turner   Hot pads   Wire cooling racks   Small narrow spatula or table knife

>>>>> recipe index

$5 Morocc[...]
Turkey Keb[...]

CREDITS
Recipe Photography
Emma Carlson and Ken Carlson

Food Stylist
Joshua Hake

Assistant Food Stylist
Trish Myers

Additional Photography
89 Getty Images/Westend61
106 C Squared Studios/Photodisc/
Getty Images
112–113 Getty Images/KidStock
Back Cover EKramer/Shutterstock;
Veniamin Kraskov/Shutterstock;
Oksana Kuzmina/Shutterstock

All other images by Shutterstock

17 Confetti Waffles

CENTENNIAL BOOKS

An Imprint of
Centennial Media, LLC
40 Worth St., 10th Floor
New York, NY 10013, U.S.A.

ISBN 978-1-951274-78-8

Distributed by
Simon & Schuster, Inc.
1230 Avenue of the Americas
New York, NY 10020, U.S.A.

For information about custom editions, special sales and premium and corporate purchases, please contact Centennial Media at contact@centennialmedia.com.

Manufactured in China

10 9 8 7 6 5 4 3 2 1

Publishers & Co-Founders Ben Harris, Sebastian Raatz
Editorial Director Annabel Vered
Creative Director Jessica Power
Executive Editor Janet Giovanelli
Features Editor Alyssa Shaffer
Deputy Editors Ron Kelly, Anne Marie O'Connor
Managing Editor Lisa Chambers
Design Director Martin Elfers
Senior Art Director Pino Impastato
Art Directors Olga Jakim, Natali Suasnavas, Joseph Ulatowski
Copy/Production Patty Carroll, Angela Taormina
Assistant Art Director Jaclyn Loney
Senior Photo Editor Jenny Veiga
Production Manager Paul Rodina
Production Assistant Alyssa Swiderski
Editorial Assistant Tiana Schippa
Sales & Marketing Jeremy Nurnberg